WHITSUN RIOT

An account of a commotion amongst
Catholics in Herefordshire and
Monmouthshire in 1605

by
Roland Mathias

BOWES & BOWES
42 Great Russell Street
LONDON

© 1963 Roland Mathias

First published in Great Britain by
BOWES & BOWES PUBLISHERS LIMITED
42 Great Russell Street, London W.C.1
and printed for the publishers by
Cox and Wyman Limited
London, Reading and Fakenham

FOREWORD

IT is perhaps significant of no more than the pitiful lack of leisure which any schoolmaster has that the collection of material for and the writing of what is no more than a minor piece of research should have taken me, off and on, the best part of twenty years. I make no apology for not having pursued the project with a more single-minded ferocity: all I can hope is that the developments in and changes of opinion which have been inevitable over so long a period do not peer independently out of the final version to the confusion of the reader.

To Balliol College, who elected me to a Schoolmaster Studentship for the Hilary Term, 1961, I owe the opportunity to prepare a definitive, if not an ultimate, typescript, and I am grateful to Mr. Christopher Hill for his advice at this stage. Among other acknowledgements which I cannot fail to make are those to Dr. B. G. Charles of The National Library of Wales, who explained for me several points of difficulty, Miss M. Jancey, of the County Library, Hereford, to whom I am indebted for one or two valuable suggestions, and Lady Mary Clive who, on a day now many years ago, was kind enough to welcome me at Whitfield.

To Mrs. B. J. George, who typed the several versions of this book and had to put up with what must have seemed an almost endless stream of emendations, I owe a deep debt of gratitude for her care and meticulous attention to detail. My thanks must go lastly, but in no sense least, to my wife, not merely for laying out two of the maps which help to elucidate the text (my son was responsible for the other), but also for the tolerance which allowed me to potter for so long to so little effect.

CONTENTS

WHITSUN RIOT

CHAPTER I

A Javelin to the Breast

IN 1605, the year of the Gunpowder Plot, there was an outbreak of violence among the Catholics in south-west Herefordshire, in the hundreds of Webtree and Wormelow close to the Monmouthshire border. For a period of approximately six weeks, from the small hours of the Tuesday morning of Whitsun week well into the month of July, a state of lawlessness persisted, a fact which may cause surprise even among those well acquainted with the period, so consistently has the evidence of it been disregarded or minimized. S. R. Gardiner in his *History of England* disposed of the matter in two sentences, and despite outline accounts in Catholic authorities like Lingard and Alexander Goss's *Introduction* to *Crosby Records*, no other non-Catholic historian until Professor A. H. Dodd has considered it worthy of attention. Yet according to Nicolo Molin, the Venetian ambassador, one of a succession of his countrymen devoted to meticulous and regular dispatches of Court gossip, King and Council were seriously afraid that in a shire so full of resolute Catholics open rebellion might be provoked. 'Council meets every day', he wrote, 'and contrary to his practice the King is present.' The perplexity of such deliberations was deepened by the feeling that force would not succeed in such a mettlesome district, while failure in a forceful policy would damage the royal reputation more seriously still. The affrays were important enough in the result to earn fresh laurels for the King's confidant, the Earl of Worcester, rapped knuckles for the Bishop

1

of Hereford and a number of magistrates, and consignment to the Tower for the alleged troublemaker-in-chief.

The story, the details of which are to be found mainly in the Salisbury Papers, the State Papers Domestic for 1605 and in a contemporary pamphlet on *The Late Commotion*, begins in the village of Allensmore, five miles south-west of Hereford,[1] just before Whitsuntide. Alice Wellington, wife of Thomas Wellington, yeoman, being but 'a simple woman, and voyd of any true grounds of Learning or Divinity', but firm in recusancy, died excommunicate and was therefore, according to subsequent Catholic apologia, refused burial by the incumbent.[2] Indignation among the Catholic community at this decision brought together a large concourse on May 21, the Tuesday of Whitsun week, very early in the morning, to bury her in the churchyard in the Papist manner. About five o'clock, an hour and a half after sunrise, Richard Heyns the vicar, lying in bed in his house adjoining the churchyard, heard the sound of a little bell, and looking out, saw some forty or fifty people, armed with swords and staves and with tapers burning, following the corpse. Before he was dressed and could prevent it, the ceremony was almost over, the body was laid in the ground, and his remonstrances were answered only with threats and revilement. Powerless, and no doubt remembering his recent admission, at the Visitation of 1604, that no sermon had been preached in Allensmore parish since the previous Christmas (and very few before that), he made what haste he could to the Bishop's Palace at Hereford and blurted out the names of those in the burial party whom he had recognized. Among the few who had caught his eye were Philip Giles of Winnall, a Monmouthshire man by birth, who carried the cross, James Coles, a weaver from Hungerstone[3] who was known to act as massing clerk to Roger Cadwallader the priest, William Chadnor, another weaver, Richard Smith, who carried the bell, William, one of the Marsh brothers of Kingstone,[4] and William Caunt of Madley. None of these were of any standing socially, except possibly Philip Giles, and however the affair was organized, the leader was not apparent.

The service was well attended by women, among whom were Joan Wellington, presumably the daughter of the deceased, and Alice Coles, wife of Coles the weaver.

Allensmore today consists of a church and a cluster of houses to the south of the Hereford–Abergavenny road and a scattering of cottages and farms to the west of it. South-eastwards, across the wide depression from which emerges the Worm Brook, is the single eminence of Aconbury Hill. To the south the skyline is complicated with hills, the tousle of heads which threaten the upper Monnow valley. Nearer, south-westwards, is the black whaleback of Treville Wood, and in the distance, emerging at either end of it, the hard, high horizon-line of the Black Mountains. Somewhere beyond Clehonger, a mile or more north and out of sight, lies the Wye. A few hundred yards north-east of Allensmore the road to Hereford begins its gradual four-mile fall down to the blur of the city suburbs.

It is the edge of anything that could be called an upper level. The land begins to roll here, but does not roll hard enough to create foothills until Treville Wood is passed. Then the rollers westward grow higher and higher, determinedly. In the shallower troughs the villages are close together, are hamlets merely and content to be out of each other's sight: Hungerstone, Winnall, Thruxton, Clehonger and Allensmore, their farms and cottages are strung out singly along the lanes, the absence of nucleation less a reminder of the confines of the old Welsh region of Ergyng than of a later and much more clearly documented poverty. For these were squatters' villages.

Perhaps because these levels were outside the main fruit-country, their sixteenth-century cottagers and hut-dwellers had known little prosperity. Rowland Vaughan of Whitehouse in Vowchurch, living no more than three miles away north-westwards in what was even then known as The Golden Valley, asserted in 1609 or 1610[5] that there were five hundred poor within a mile and a half of his house who got some sort of a living ostensibly by spinning flax and hemp, but had not five shillings to buy a bale to work with. Instead, they begged, pillaged the orchards and gardens, and gleaned in the fields. As many as three hundred leazers or gleaners had been seen in one gentleman's cornfield at once. It was indeed a poor country, scraping deferentially towards the manor houses of Arkston, Poston, New Court and White-house, and getting little enough. J. P. Malcolm, who visited the south-east end of The Golden Valley in the first decade of the nineteenth century, found the visual beauty of the scene still dis-figured by great numbers of tumbledown huts, wretchedly con-structed of clay and sods and branches, which, with vegetable patches and animal-runs, proliferated among the waste on either side of the road. The squatters had evidently gleaned their way through ten generations.

Whether it would be justifiable to see a connection between so high a population in an area apparently agricultural and the pre-valence of recusancy is much more open to doubt. Certainly a region that was 'plentifullest of poor in the kingdom' lies open to the suspicion that it was made so by incomers, that it was, for various reasons, known to be *safe* for Catholics. This suspicion, in so far as it referred to persons of higher economic standing and to the county as a whole, was voiced by the Bishop of Hereford after the riots had begun. But there is little real evidence about the poor of Dore and Hungerstone, or of why they were thereabouts in such numbers. If we follow Robert Reyce, author of *The Breviary of Suffolk*, published in 1618, in his opinion that 'where the clothiers do dwell or have dwelt, there are found the greatest number of poor'[6] and observe in what Rowland Vaughan called 'the Garden of Old Gallants and Paradice of the backside of the Principallitie'[7] a great many spinners of flax and hemp and more than the usual complement of weavers, we are still only guessing after what we do not yet know. There were instances of gavelkind inheritance in Archenfield as late as 1600, and it may well be that the dire poverty of so many of the inhabitants of Dore and Bacton and Vowchurch is traceable to the equal division of property among the children of a deceased yeoman which this Welsh land law compelled.

In any case, the connection between poverty and Catholicism remains unproven. The Marches of Wales were throughout their length conservatively and Catholicly inclined and, even if Rowland Vaughan were exaggerating to his own credit in asserting that there were 'not two sermons in the Golden Vale this 500 years', had not been well served by the Elizabethan Church. Probably the residual influence of the Abbey of Dore, dissolved over sixty years before, was at least as strong, except in crisis, as the injunction of the Bishop, and a few, at least, of the local poor may have been maintained by it.

The recusant belt, which the disturbances of 1605 highlight, stretched from Sugwas, north of Wye, where the Bishop's palace had been in the thirteenth century, and Whitecross, where the saintly Thomas de Cantilupe[8] rested on his journeys between Sugwas and Hereford, through Allensmore (of which John Seabourne of Sutton St. Michael, a well-known Catholic,[9] was landlord) southwards through Kilpeck, Dore and Wormbridge to Skenfrith, Garway and Llanrothal in the valley of the Monnow. Mass was regularly said at The Darren, upstream from Llanrothal, by Father Robert Jones, who in 1609 became Superior of the English Jesuits, and at Whitfield in Treville Park by Roger Cadwallader, the seminary priest who was martyred at Leominster in 1610. Upon these two centres turned the axis of events.

Across the forgotten boundary of Ergyng, on May 24, three days after the burial of Alice Wellington, came George Wenlond, High Constable of the Hundred, with a warrant from the Bishop of Hereford to seize those whom the Vicar of Allensmore had named. He and his aides made first for the little hamlet of Hungerstone, an undulation or two west of the churchyard where the burial had taken place. There they arrested James Coles and William Chadnor,[10] weavers who worked in adjoining rooms. But neither submitted without a struggle. First Chadnor escaped, and some of the posse pursued him for a distance without success. Then in their absence Coles, picking up 'a short knife, which Weavers commonly use to cut off their threads' wounded

    [6] Quoted in Christopher Hill, *The Century of Revolution*, p. 25.

    [7] Op. cit., p. 36.

    [8] Bishop of Hereford, 1275–82. Canonized forty years later.

    [9] His wife Sibyl was named at Christmas 1604 as one of the principal and most dangerous recusants in the County.

    [10] Or Thomas. Both William and Thomas Chadnor were present at the funeral: and since *The Late Commotion* gives no Christian name, only the fact that William appears early on the list in the State Papers cited and was evidently one of the more important actors in the affair inclines the choice in his favour.

    [11] Described as 'a gentleman' and referred to as 'Master William Gough', he had evidently accompanied the High Constable.

    [12] Of Kingstone, the brother of William Marsh already referred to. *The Late Commotion* asserts that he 'had likewise beene in the former Action, and was also one of the men named in the Warrant'. The vicar's list (*S.P.* 14, Vol. XIV, 53), however, mentions William but not Leonard, and since the extant list is a later copy, states specifically that William was at that time in custody. Leonard was then in custody also, and his omission from the list is probably no accident. If, as is surmised, Leonard's name was either not included in the warrant or mistakenly included, it would explain why he risked entering the weavers' shop to help his friends. An error of this sort may have served too as a basis of legal protest.

    [13] He was one of those early in custody, and like a number of others who appeared before the Bishop of Hereford and Paul Delahay, was very earnest then to clear himself of all blame. Like several others in this narrative he was married to a wife whose Catholicism outran his own. The name of Katherine Philipps, wife of John Philipps of Dewchurch, was cited in the list of the most dangerous recusants in the county, compiled at Christmas 1604. She was formerly Katherine Lewis of Kivernoll: John Philipps obtained the estate by his marriage to her.

    [14] This is conjectural: Morgan 'came only to speake a word or two with him', according to *The Late Commotion*, which was unlikely to admit an official error. But whoever Morgan was he would have been foolish to quarrel with the execution of the law thus openly unless he had some legal ground. That Leonard had been mistaken for William Marsh was probably that ground.

CHAPTER II

The Recusant Problem: King's Move or Bishop's?

R̲ɪᴏᴛ and forcible rescue, these were now fact and incontrovertible. But if the offence was certain, the remedy was not. *The Late Commotion*, concerned to put white immediately on black, asserted that Sir Herbert Croft, of Croft Castle near Shobdon in the north of the county, was sent down from London to initiate an inquiry and to hold up the Bishop's hands until it should be plainer what the proportions of the trouble were. Sir Herbert, in 1605 much more active than the senior member of Parliament for the County, Sir Thomas Coningsby of Hampton, whose years and bulk had for some time made travelling a trial,[1] had all but recovered the prestige and independence of his grandfather Sir James, who had been senior knight of the shire in every Parliament from 1563 to 1589 and had, up to his death in 1590, been almost the only influential person to oppose the growth of the successive Leicester and Pembroke factions in Wales and the Marches. The political attitude of the Crofts seems to have remained constant: up to February 1601 Sir Herbert was known as one of the friends and supporters of the Earl of Essex. He does not appear immediately to have incurred disfavour with Sir Robert Cecil, however, who the following month supported his application for the Stewardship of Leominster against that of Sir Thomas Coningsby, who had been nominated by the Bailiff and Deputy Recorder of the Borough. The same year he was nominated to serve on the

9

Council in the Marches, one of the few suggested by Justice Henry Townshend whom Cecil ultimately accepted.

However easily the younger County member might get the better of Sir Thomas Coningsby, his immobile senior, and settle by mere survival the Croft-Coningsby feud of years, he ultimately embarked upon a course of opposition to the extent of the jurisdiction of the Council in the Marches and the authority of its President which Cecil was bound to interpret as overt opposition to himself. Early in May 1603 something had 'passed from him to discontent' the Earl of Salisbury, and, although he was knighted at Theobalds on the 7th of the month, this honour was his only as a result of a special plea made on his behalf by the Earl of Southampton, who urged that Croft's action 'proceeded rather from his present grief than out of any want of respect'. In a letter written in 1617 (when he went into retirement and exile in France) he acknowledged that, both in James's first Parliament and subsequently, he had petitioned against the jurisdiction of the Council in the Marches over Herefordshire, and that his Majesty had 'stood ill conceyted' of him in consequence. Worcestershire and Herefordshire, the counties least represented numerically on the Council,[2] had as early as 1597 formed an alliance with the metropolitan lawyers, who served the Assize Courts and resented the Council's interferences, to oppose the influence of the President. By 1603 this alliance had resolved itself more clearly: Sir Herbert Croft and Sir John Packington spoke for the gentry of the dissident counties and behind them were arrayed the lawyers of the King's Bench under Sir Edward Coke. Lord Zouche, President of the Council since Pembroke's death, was both isolated and ailing: he persistently requested his release from duty. But he was Salisbury's nominee, and any flouting of his authority was felt at Hatfield. His instructions were to stick it out.

It is necessary to consider Sir Herbert Croft's position in this way because his coming down to Herefordshire on the command of the Privy Council has about it at first an air of unlikelihood.

Was he the man, as late as 1605, to command the Council's confidence? Was his own stance in religion orthodox enough and acceptable both to the King and the Bishop of Hereford? Certainly, in the Essex alliance, he had been a collaborator, if at a distance, with recusant squires. Certainly, too, his sister Mary was married to John Davies of Hereford, writing-master, versifier and Catholic. The ultimate oddity is, though this was not to be foreseen in 1605, that for the last five years of his life (and he was no more than fifty-six at death) he became a monk in the Benedictine community at Douai. But such evidence is insufficient to convict him of being a sympathizer with recusancy in 1605. In family terms the religious position was extremely confused. Hardly a significant border family but had its recusant branch. Hardly a justice of the peace but had a recusant wife or mother or sister. Sir Herbert was less an equivocator than most and was clearly, between 1602 and 1605, an opponent, in the competitive interests of the County, of the pro-Catholic Bodenham-Morgan-Baskerville group. Independent as he was, indeed, he little deserves Professor J. E. Neale's verdict on him as 'having no distinction but that of family'.[3]

Chief Justice Popham's commendation of him in 1603 as 'very honest . . . and very sure . . . to be trusted' evidently still carried some weight with Salisbury, who noted also his readiness, as a member of the Council in the Marches, to work against what might appear an interest of his own. Whatever the reason for his dispatch to Herefordshire (and it may have been only a hasty and stopgap measure), Sir Herbert was nothing if not direct. On his arrival in the county, according to *The Late Commotion*,[4] some of the justices suspected of Catholic leanings were put out of the Commission of the Peace, and 'certayne gentlemen' were sent up to London to answer the matter. It is nevertheless strange that neither the Bishop of Hereford nor any other commentator makes any reference to Sir Herbert's presence or to his summary measures. Possibly his dispatch from London represented on the part of the Council a primary and straightforward intention to answer

violence with stern repressive action. If so, this mood was soon
to change.

A letter from a Catholic relative to Sir Everard Digby of
Cotehurst, Buckinghamshire, who was later inculpated in the
Gunpowder Plot, reported that the King made a three-hour speech
to the robed judges at the Court of Greenwich on Sunday, June 9,
in the course of which he made it plain that there was no longer
any need to spare the blood of recusants and that the Herefordshiremen should serve for example. This was evidently the way the
matter was to be represented publicly. The Venetian ambassador,
however, writing on June 15, reported the Council as very loath
to use force in the King's name for fear of provoking a general
rising. It would be better, they thought, to dissemble until they
could get ten or twelve of the rebel leaders into their hands.
Meanwhile the magistrates of the county should be instructed to
use every means at their disposal to trap such leaders, acting upon
the authority they already held, and not upon any special warrant
of the King or Council. The decision to pass this unwelcome buck
downwards was justified, naïvely enough, on the ground that a
royal warrant would have to be carried out with greater severity.
Plainly, however, for the *Council* to do *nothing* was to prolong the
absence of adequate pronouncement and information, to perpet-
uate the time-lag between an evolving royal policy and its re-
quirements in propaganda – a costive deficiency which had been
one of the main causes of the Herefordshire commotion, as it had
been of Watson's Plot previously. Sir Henry Neville was perhaps
not far wrong in his opinion, penned on June 21, that 'It seems the
Rule is here forgotten, *d'estre ou tout bon ou tout mauvais*, and that
this *via di mezzo* is ever the worst'.

Meanwhile, the Bishop and the magistrates were in a most un-
fortunate position. Without additional assistance either of force
or authority they were to pursue a course of whose deficiencies
they were aware and whose failure they could foretell, and at the
same time accept the responsibility for that failure. Lack of firmness and the spreading of false rumours of the King's personal

desire for toleration had, in the Bishop's opinion, emboldened the recusants to rebellion. How should that same feebleness, uncorrected publicly, be expected to restore order? For the unhappy executants of such a policy (if policy it could be called) there lay ahead either disobedience or failure, neither of them eminently cheerful in consequence.

Perhaps of them all the Bishop had least hope of disposing of the matter with unburnt fingers. A native of Baldock, Hertfordshire, Robert Bennett had been at one time Master of the great Hospital of St. Cross at Winchester, but had despoiled it in order to buy himself preferment to the Deanery of Windsor. In this simony he was no whit different from the majority of the clerics of his time, among whom Lancelot Andrewes was very much the exception in twice refusing promotion to a bishopric[5] because the price of acceptance was the assignment of a portion of the episcopal revenues to the Crown. By sedulous petitioning and the active support of Archbishop Whitgift, who told Cecil that he could not think 'of fitter persons for Hereford than . . . the Bishop of Chester and Dr. Bennett, Dean of Windsor,' he had then obtained the vacant bishopric and was consecrated on February 20, 1603. Advancement, however, had brought not so much greater satisfaction as greater political danger. Hereford was a key bishopric. The interpretation of James's tortuous policy towards the Catholics could not be there, as at Ely or Peterborough, a matter of the merest academic interest. It was an eel as live as any in Wye, to be caught, measured and put back each week. Before long Dr. Bennett was dispiritedly complaining, not merely of the frequent miscarriage of letters, but also of 'this cold and rheumatic place where I now live'.

Sir John Harington had described him when at Trinity College, Cambridge, as 'an active man, who played well at tennis, and could toss an argument in the schools even better than a ball in the tennis-court'. But personal qualities of a different sort were needed in his new bishopric. What little evidence there is reveals him as a vain, contentious individual, who spent large sums on the restoration of his palace, delighted in the sight of his coat of arms on the fronts of Hereford houses[6] and quarrelled about his 'liberties' with the City Council.[7] Even his demonstrations of zeal were not well-chosen. He was remembered by one Catholic novice,[8] admittedly a hostile witness, as 'the odious prelate' who in the early months of 1605 summoned him, in company with about a dozen of his friends, out of the Cathedral school, and failing to bully them into a promise of conformity, sent for the schoolmaster and had them expelled. Such tactics as these were not likely to weaken the Catholic position.

And yet it is hard not to be sorry for Bennett. He had no claim to be a Cantilupe, venerated as a saint because he had enlarged the bishop's prerogative,[9] nor a constitutionally detached academician like Lancelot Andrewes. He was just a political bishop with the political game going against him, and a hand strong only in clubs.

Moreover, to minimize the Catholic problem in his diocese would be unfair. In Hereford itself, at his very doors, recusant meetings were held. A few months after King James's accession about a hundred and forty people were discovered in the act of celebrating the Feast of the Purification of the Blessed Virgin Mary. On February 2, 1604 some thirty more, many of them citizens of standing, were detected at mass in the house of John Ireland. A feature of these occasions was the faithfulness of the Catholic womenfolk, not a few of them widows: time-serving and placeholding among the men, inevitably, were far more common: whether from conviction or uxoriousness, however, they did follow at a distance the greater daring of their wives. Much use was made of the services of physicians, whose ease of movement among the population made them valuable messengers and liaison officers with the more outlying sections of the Catholic community. One of the more threatening contemporary developments, as the Bishop was not slow to point out, was a species of congregation of recusants from Lancashire and Yorkshire, Oxfordshire, Berkshire, Gloucestershire, Warwickshire, Somer-

set and Dorset into the neighbourhood of Hereford, either because
of the greater immunity they enjoyed there on account of numbers or because, in terms of some wider Jesuit strategy, there really
was something afoot. Whichever was the case, the Bishop could
afford to look glum.

One group among these immigrants calls for special comment.
In Hereford town itself there was no more persistent Catholic
than Jane Griffiths, wife of Ambrose Griffiths, a lawyer, and
mother of the boy who was dragged from the Cathedral school
to answer the Bishop's questions.[10] Ambrose himself was 'an halfe
Recusant and a dangerous man . . . said to bee of Glamorganshire'.
Undoubtedly this was the third son of Hugh Griffiths of Penmark,[11]
one of the six Clerks in Chancery in Elizabeth's reign. A bencher
of Lincoln's Inn, he had been discharged from the Fleet by Wal-
singham in July 1582 upon bond of a hundred pounds to conform,
and he was evidently still exercising the care of one who could
judge the consequences. Interesting as Ambrose and Jane Griffiths
may be, however, they are not of themselves alone significant.
But joined by a high proportion, if not the whole, of the considerable Penmark family, who had appeared in Herefordshire as
in the promised land, they become a portent. Ambrose had arrived
from Gloucestershire soon after 1591. His eldest brother William
had settled at The Cwm, Llanrothal, one of the two focal points
of disturbance in June and July 1605. There too, or in the same
parish, lived his sister Jane, the widow of Rowland Watson of
London, who had reassumed her maiden name. Both she and her
son John Watson were rich and, like William Griffiths, firmly
Catholic.[12] It is possible, even probable, that James Griffiths, the
second in age of the Penmark brothers, a doctor of medicine and
a Catholic, was likewise resident in Llanrothal at The Cwm, but
the evidence is conflicting and the problem is not made easier by
frequent confusions over Christian names.[13] Richard Griffiths, the
youngest of all the brothers,[14] was a Jesuit. Known alternatively as
Fleming, his mother's name, or Watson, that of his sister, he was
frequently to be found at The Cwm and, although he died in

1607, lived long enough to arrange a passage for his nephew James, Ambrose's son, to the College at St. Omer, and ultimately, in November 1611, to the English College at Rome.[15] Northward at Arkston, near the cockpit of violence, was Elizabeth, sister to William, James, Ambrose and Richard and widow of Thomas Morgan of Arkston. Her son, Sir Charles Morgan, was lord of the manor of Treville and justice of the peace for the county, a man whose weight and position will require exact discussion. One of Sir Charles's sisters, Katherine, the fifth child of Elizabeth Morgan (née Griffiths), had married William Gwillim of Tregate in Llanrothal, so swelling by one more the number of the Griffiths family in that part of the Monnow valley.

These dispositions were comprehensive, however initially fortuitous. But they do not exhaust the possibilities of the tribe of Griffiths. Two of the brothers, John the fourth and Hugh the fifth, are not known to have been in Herefordshire or Monmouthshire in 1605. Of the latter nothing is known beyond the fact that he, like Richard, was a Jesuit. But there were no fewer than three persons of the name of John Griffiths who had some share in the disturbances, one a drover, one a grazier, and the third a gentleman recusant of Kingstone. One of these, probably the last, was important enough to merit the specific attention of the authorities when the hunt was up.[16] This John might have been held to be of the family of Penmark were it not that the declaration made at Rome in 1611 by the young James Griffiths, from which most of our information derives, omitted all mention of him. If John Griffiths of Penmark were in the area and a fervent Catholic, this would be cause indeed for surprise, since in James's account even schismatic relatives were detailed. It would be even more intriguing were there any proof that Rice Griffiths, the conforming priest at whose door much of the blame for the Allensmore riot was subsequently laid, was a member of this widespread family. But the balance of evidence is against it.[17]

The ramifications of the Penmark family are not perhaps immediately relevant. But the geographical distribution of the

Catholics concerned in the troubles of 1605 is oddly distinctive, the list of participants denuded of rank and brief. The presence of the children of Hugh Griffiths at both ends of the axis of disturbance may be held to have had a relation to the degree of organization demonstrated among the rebels, though whether that relation was of a positive or negative nature it is too early to determine.

The remainder of the recusant population of the area is also not without interest. Hereford itself was one focus. There Michael Vaughan, one of the Vaughans of Hergest, attended Church but ran 'the Jesuit courses most violently'. Dr. Harley, a lawyer and physician resident in Hereford, was one of the links with Catholics outside the city and was frequently to be found at William Morgan's house at Treville Park. The Bishop called him 'a simple doctor, made beyond seas', whose 'doctorship has carried away the simple people long'. In particular it was alleged that 'the better to insinuate himself into company he practises physic'. The brothers Edward and Gregory Havard were 'most hott for the Jesuits, especially Gregorye';[18] the house of Richard and Edward Clarke at Wellington, four miles north of the city, was one of their favourite resorts. There, too, went William Ely, Vice-President of St. John's College, Oxford, from 1559 to 1563, but since deprivation a secular priest in Hereford, who, although supposedly a prisoner, 'rideth upp and downe the contrey as hee liste'. This man was feared even by his co-religionists for his strict morals and harsh integrity, having earned some kind of distinction by refusing his hand to Cranmer as a relapsed heretic when the latter was going to the stake.[19] He was regarded by his opponents as dangerous, particularly perhaps because in his custody were some reputed relics of St. Thomas Cantilupe, guaranteed to spur the fervour of local Catholics. Ultimately these relics passed to the Clarkes.

At Wellington, too, was to be found Paul Spence, alias Peters, another old priest reputedly 'as hott for the Jesuits as any', who divided his time between the home of the Clarkes and that of Thomas Bridges, a few miles west at Sugwas.[20] But Spence was not personally, as was Ely, a danger to be reckoned with: in December 1586 he had 'subscribed to the Queen's supreme authority in all causes'²¹ and was likely, under pressure, to surrender again. Farther north at Bromyard, occasional visitors at the house of John Abington, cofferer to Queen Elizabeth, and his son Thomas, the antiquary (whose younger brother had been executed for his part in the Babington Plot), were the two Jesuits Lister, alias Butler,²² and Oldcorne, alias Hall, the latter of whom was subsequently caught in the toils of the Gunpowder Plot. Both these were more normally resident on the main Abington estate at Hindlip Hall, Worcestershire, where they were doubtless the Bishop of Worcester's scourge. Lister, however, who was confessor to Mistress Dorothy Abington, sister to Thomas, and inhabited a separate part of Hindlip Hall, appears to have been free to take a hand in Herefordshire when the occasion merited it. The commotion of 1605 may have been such an occasion.

So far, however, the Catholics listed have been recusants, but not actively involved in the violence of May and June 1605. With the exception of Dr. Harley, the Hereford physician, and the Jesuit Lister, none of them moved from the wings on to the stage.

The real actors were few, confined both in place and station. It is to them that we must look next.

¹ He went to Parliament in 1601 'as God knows, much against my will; which journey I am to perform in coach, being altogether unable to mount a horse'. J. E. Neale, *The Elizabethan House of Commons*, pp. 34–5.

² Between 1560 and 1603 these two counties had only six members each, in comparison with seventeen from Gloucestershire and twenty-two from Shropshire. The Council normally sat, moreover, either at Ludlow or Shrewsbury. Penry Williams, *The Council in the Marches of Wales under Elizabeth I*, p. 204.

³ Op. cit. pp. 34–5.

⁴ Ostensibly in a letter written on June 29.

⁵ The bishoprics in question were Salisbury and Ely, offered him by Queen

Elizabeth. Andrewes was ultimately made Bishop of Chichester in 1605 by James, without conditions. His reputation as a saintly man has suffered at the hands of modern critics, however: e.g. Trevor-Roper, *Archbishop Laud*, pp. 30–1: 'Andrewes was a man after James's own heart: one who, in the serene detachment of an assured position and a clear conscience, displayed his learning and advanced his theories without disturbing the world by any dangerous attempt to apply them.'

⁶ The arms of the See were three leopards' heads reversed, swallowing as many fleurs-de-lis or, on a field gules. Guillim, *A Display of Heraldrie*, p. 180.

⁷ There was a serious dispute with the Mayor and Aldermen in May 1607.

⁸ James Griffiths, alias Grafton, son of Ambrose Griffiths.

⁹ The Archbishop of Canterbury asserted, however, that the King had restored to Dr. Bennett (as to the Bishop of Norwich) all the mesne profits arising in the vacancy of his bishopric. *Cal. of Salis. MSS.*, XVI, p. 407 (1604).

¹⁰ *S.P.* 14, Vol. XIV, 53. James Griffiths, who entered the English College, Rome, on November 7, 1611, stated that it was through the care and industry of his mother that he was reconciled to the Church of Rome 'by a certain priest of Hereford, now dead, named Mr. Williams' (probably Parry, alias Williams. *S.P.* 14, Vol. XIV, 40). Foley, op. cit., Vol. IV, p. 429. His testimony, however, raises one serious difficulty: he gave his mother's name as Jane Thompson (alive in 1611). The Sheriff's Lists are firm in twice referring to her as *Lucy* Griffiths, and the dates make it clear that Ambrose was not married twice.

¹¹ By Ann Fleming of Flimston. G. T. Clark, *Limbus Patrum Morganiae et Glamorganiae*, p. 146. Ann Fleming was his third wife.

¹² This and the preceding statement are inferences from the presence in Llanrothal, next in order of precedence among recusants, of a Jane Griffiths, widow (Duncumb, *Continuation: Hundred of Wormelow*, Lower Division, Part II, John Hobson Matthews), and several persons of the name of Watson or Whetson, a name unusual in those parts. John Griffiths, alias Whetson, yeoman, was next in order of precedence among recusants in Llanrothal to William Griffiths of the Cwm and his wife. *S.P.* 14, Vol. XIV, 53, gives John Watson and Sara Watson. James Griffiths (Foley, op. cit., Vol. IV, p. 429) gives his cousin's name, curiously, as *William* Watson, a name which does not occur in the official lists, though there was a William Watkins, gentleman recusant of Llanrothal.

¹³ The list of dangerous recusants at Christmas 1604 (*S.P.* 14, Vol. XIV, 53) contains the name of James Griffiths of Llanrothal and Mary his wife: but since these appear first, to the exclusion of William Griffiths (whose wife's name was also Mary), it may reasonably be inferred that a substitution of Christian names has taken place. Again, John Griffiths, 'a Phisition . . . that goeth much abroade to Gentlemens houses' (*S.P.* 14, Vol. XIV, 40), may have been none other than James, M.D., since he is mentioned immediately between William Griffiths of The Cwm and Ambrose Griffiths. Although there is no other reference to this John Griffiths the 'Phisition', the position is complicated by the presence in the region of a possible three other persons named John Griffiths.

[14] Clark, op. cit., p. 146, gave Rees as the name of the sixth and youngest son. James Griffiths, however (Foley, op. cit., Vol. IV, p. 429), confirmed that he had an uncle named Richard Griffiths who was a member of the Society of Jesus.

[15] Having completed his course in philosophy, James intended entering the novitiate of the Society at Louvain, but on his journey there died of a fever at Bologna.

[16] *Cal. of Salis. MSS.*, Part XVII, p. 258. Bishop of Hereford to Earl of Salisbury, June 13, 1605: 'Roger Cadwallader will not yet be found, nor Rice ap Rice, nor John Griffithes.'

[17] The possibility arises only because Clark, op. cit., p. 146, gave Rees, not Richard, as the name of the sixth son of Hugh Griffiths. In view of the connection of the Griffiths family with the Jesuits, however, and the anti-Jesuit tendencies of the priest, Rice Griffiths, such an identification is unlikely. Little is known of the Jesuit Richard except that he was born in Bangor in 1576, studied at the English College, Rome, entered the novitiate of St. Andrew, Rome, on May 25, 1594 and died in London in 1607. (Father C. Grene's Collection, C. p. 206, cited in Foley.) But his existence as a separate personality seems to be established.

[18] Of Pipley. The Havards were evidently a strongly Catholic family, for Alice, daughter of Thomas Havard of Hereford and possibly a sister of Edward and Gregory, married Thomas Bowen of Kimbolton, a few miles north-east of Leominster, and afterwards of Trefloyne, Tenby. In both these places she was noted for recusancy, and was excommunicated for it at the Pembrokeshire Autumn Sessions of 1613. *Vide* Francis Jones, op. cit.

[19] Foley, op. cit., Vol. IV, p. 454. Dodd's *Church History*, cited there, refers to this as 'primitive behaviour' and continues: 'This nicety has been represented by some as either humour or a want of charity; but others have regarded it as an instance of his zeal, and very agreeable to the letter of the Scriptures.'

[20] Bridges 'goeth sometymes to the Churche, yet is hee Jesuite in high degree. His wiffe is a Recusante.' *S.P.* 14, Vol. XIV, 53, refers to Thomas and Katherine Bridges as of Eaton Bishop, but the parish of Eaton traditionally included Sugwas, although the Wye flows between (cf. Blount of Orleton).

[21] He was committed to the Fleet on December 29, 1585. In December 1586 his was the only name (among those of many priests and laymen seized at the time of the Babington Plot) against which was recorded an indication of complete submission. Cath. Rec. Soc. Miscellanea, II, pp. 246 and 272.

[22] Formerly with Richard Cotton of Warblington, Hampshire (*Cal. of Salis. MSS.*, Part XVII, p. 500. Thomas Wilson to Earl of Salisbury, November 20, 1605, giving the haunts of Jesuits 'a good while since'): but he must have become an *operarius* in the Marches of Wales before the death of Queen Elizabeth, since he was alleged to have attempted at that time to urge the men of Worcestershire to arms to follow the supposed example of the Herefordshiremen. *S.P.* 14, Vol. XIV, 40.

CHAPTER III

Priests, Magistrates and Intelligencers

THE real lines of secrecy, necessarily connected as they were with Hereford, whence both news and threats of trouble might be expected, ran not north but west and south-west, up the Wye to Sugwas and Eaton Bishop, along the Abergavenny road to Allensmore, Hungerstone, Treville, Kilpeck, Dore and Wormbridge, and down the valley of the Monnow by way of Garway, Skenfrith and Llanrothal. Recusancy in this last region was reputedly a flame fanned by Robert Jones, 'the Fyerbrande of all', who had been officially reported some years earlier both at the house of Mr. Dracot at Paynsley in Shropshire and with the Morgans of Llantarnam.[1] Born in 1564 near Chirk, and known variously as Holland, Hilarius, or Hay, he had been from 1590 to 1595 (when he arrived in England) Professor of Philosophy at the English College in Rome. A man of superior intellect and real learning, he was the chosen instrument of the Counter-Reformation in Wales, nominated for the work by Father Robert Parsons, Prefect of the English Jesuit Mission, and having under his immediate direction a number of seminary priests, of whom the most significant were Reginald (or Robert) Eaton, alias North (for whom he has been mistaken),[2] and James Morris, alias Jones. In 1609 he succeeded Father Holtby as Superior of the whole Jesuit order in Britain, a position which he held until his death in 1615. By 1605, having established his organization in both North and South Wales, he was a regular visitor at The Cwm, Llanrothal, the house of William Griffiths, and not infrequently said mass, either in company with or in alternation with another Jesuit named William Powell, like himself a native of North Wales,[3] at The Darren, some two miles off. James Morris, alias Jones, already referred to, who in the year or so previous had several times accompanied converts to the seminaries at Douai and Valladolid, was also particularly associated with The Darren. Whether this Morris was, in the weeks of the uprising of 1605, a 'Jesuited priest' in the sense used in the Sheriff's List must be discussed later.

In choosing Llanrothal for one of his massing-places, Father Robert Jones was probably moved both by the residual strength of Catholicism in the immediate vicinity and by the inaccessibility of that part of the valley of the Monnow, factors which are plainly interrelated. The Cwm, much more notorious in 1679 as the recently discovered Jesuit College of St. Francis Xavier, stood high on the eastern side of the valley, at the edge of a deep recession well away from the river. Any movement from the south-west or south, from the direction of Monmouth, could be seen a long way off. Behind the house woods climbed steeply to the crown of the hill, woods in which during the frenzy aroused by the Popish Plot the Protestant searchers uncovered the exits of several underground passages leading away from The Cwm.[4] No priests, it had been intended, should lightly there be taken.

The Darren was even more successfully hidden. Nowadays the depopulation of the neighbourhood has resulted in the extinction of almost all oral tradition about it. This part of the Monnow valley is a region dotted with ruined farms and cottages. Darren Wood, Darren Cottage[5] and Darren Mill are all to be found on the ordnance map, but their presence is confusing rather than helpful. The absence of any house called The Darren from a map of the parish of Skenfrith,[6] made in Henry VIII's reign, suggests that it was of no great size or standing, as indeed the denial of the title of 'gent' to William Walker, its occupant of 1605, would indicate. A map in the Hereford City Library, dated 1698,[7] is more enlightening. From this it would seem that The Darren may be identified either with a cottage nowadays called The Sand House, or with one of several other nearby cottages now in ruins, all of them some four hundred yards from the main Skenfrith–Ross road and separated from it by a sharp elbow of valley. Opposite, westwards, stands Coed Anghred Hill. In the height of summer the Darren Wood shadows the eastern bank of the Monnow and the shallows, of recent years, are massed with Indian balsam. From the south the site is invisible until the last moment. Eastward and up the hill the narrow dingle is deep in fern and the trees meet again a few hundred feet away. In this forest hamlet lived William Walker and somewhere in the three roods of ground still known in 1698 as Chapel Pleck stood the building where mass was regularly said by James Morris, alias Jones, the resident priest, and at intervals by either Robert Jones or William Powell. A little distance northwards, no more than a step from these wood-encircled cottages, was St. Michael's Well (more commonly known as The Priest's Well) about which oral tradition is still strong, but whose continuing spring now trickles ignominiously through a pipe.

Among the strategic considerations of recusancy must also have been the fact that the river here constitutes the boundary between two dioceses. Skenfrith and Coed Anghred opposite were subject to the Bishop of Llandaff, and a quick change of episcopal overlord could hardly do less than earn a temporary respite. If there be any truth in the story that the Bishops of Hereford and Llandaff went out together in June 1605 after the recusants then in arms, the reason is not far to seek.

A more serious problem is raised by the close and apparent relation between this area of the middle Monnow and the first centre of disturbance at Allensmore, Hungerstone and Treville Park. At a time when the outbreak received little or no support from Catholics in other and contiguous neighbourhoods, the solidarity in rebellion of the men of The Darren, separated as they were from Treville by a dozen miles or more, was most marked. It will be impossible at this stage even to indicate an answer to this problem, but the more northerly area plainly deserves an examination at least as careful as that accorded to Llanrothal.

c

Undoubtedly the most constant influence upon Catholics in Allensmore, Hungerstone, Thruxton, Winnall, Treville, Wormbridge and Kilpeck was that of Roger Cadwallader, the seminary priest, although another and more ephemeral priestly character named Edwards was heard of in those parishes from time to time. Cadwallader, alias Rogers, was born in 1567, three years later than Robert Jones, at Stretton Sugwas, just across the Wye to the north of the district of his ministry, and according to the brief account of him given by Bishop Challoner, his greatest claims to distinction were his excellence in Greek and a rare talent for controversy. As in so many of the briefer hagiographies, however, the manner of his death outruns in print anything he achieved while living. He was seized by James Prichard, the under-sheriff, at the house of a widow named Mrs. Winifred Scroope, eight miles out of Hereford, on Easter Day, 1610, and martyred at Leominster on August 27 following, one of four priests, three seculars and one regular, who suffered that year.[8] In 1605, however, he was a man of thirty-eight years of age, in the very prime of his ministry. Such name as he had made for himself had been as an uncompromising opponent of the Jesuits. In 1600 he had been amongst the appellants to Rome in the great Archpriest controversy. In January 1603 he had been one of fifteen secular priests who made a written profession of allegiance to the King, reserving only their religion and the use of their priestly functions, and delivered it by four of their number to Richard Bancroft, then Bishop of London, in response to his previous overture by proclamation.[9] It does not appear that Roger Cadwallader, any more than the other eleven, ever made his submission in person; but his political position was very like, in all but the overweening personal vanity, that of the ill-fated William Watson with whose revolt he was probably associated.[10] He was certainly to be counted among the 'English party'.

Cadwallader, for some time before the outbreak with which we are concerned, had regularly said mass at Whitfield in Treville Park. A bald statement of this sort, however, may give rise to serious misconceptions. The modern Whitfield, with its two-mile-long drive from the southern lodge on the Hereford–Abergavenny road, its walled garden and extensive lawns, not to mention the height and solidity of the house itself, is the early nineteenth-century creation of the heirs of Edward Bolton Clive, who bought the property in 1798. The Whitfield of the late sixteenth and early seventeenth centuries was probably not more than a farmhouse of some pretension, and between 1549 and 1560 it was occupied by John Gwillim, eldest son and heir of Gwillim of Cillwch in the parish of Hentland, four or five miles south-east. By 1569 this John was home and in possession at Cillwch, and of who occupied Whitfield subsequently there is no sign. Probably, in any case, it was not William Morgan. In 1617 a grant of the manors of Kilpeck and Treville made mention of 'the farm called the Parke wherein William Morgan, gent, dwells'. The interval of twelve years between the disturbances of 1605 and the utterance of this deed makes caution necessary; it is entirely possible that one of the conditions upon which Morgan was ultimately released from the Tower was that he cease to reside at 'the farm called Whitefield otherwise Dayerie otherwise Hopleas'. But without further evidence there seems no reason to believe that he ever did so reside.

Treville had been at the time of the Domesday Survey a royal forest of over 2,000 acres, and despite its subsequent subjection to Alayn de Plunkenet, who in 1299 styled himself Lord of Kilpeck Castle and of the Forest of Treville, and a number of equally rapacious successors, had continued as an extra-parochial liberty, whose status in the early seventeenth century was very partially understood. In 1610, in the course of the hearing before an Ex-chequer Commission at Grosmont of a complaint preferred by John Gwillim, clerk, against Sir Charles Morgan of Arkston,[11] evidence was taken as to whether there had been, at some previous time, a chapel in Treville Park. Opinion was divided: but some, at least, of the yeomen resident there claimed to have heard of one. One went so far as to affirm that the site of it was at Park Orles.[12] Tithes had apparently belonged to the Abbey of Gracedieu,

Monmouth, before the Dissolution, but recent rights of collection were much less certain. One deponent alleged that as late as 1574 tithes had been paid to the parson of Thruxton by householders in Treville Park to entitle them to attend divine service in Thruxton parish. It was apparent that there was a deal of mystery about many points which in an ordinary parish were clearly defined, and the phrase of one witness, who spoke of the Park as 'sometimes called a wild forest', reveals that the medieval name and status of a Forest were no longer locally understood. Manorial lordship in 1605 was, however, undoubtedly exercised from Arkston. In 1613 a ninety-nine-year lease previously granted by Sir Charles Morgan, then head of the Arkston household, was assigned by John James of Kilpeck to Sir Walter Pye of The Mynde. In 1617 the manor of Treville, its woods and farms,[13] was granted outright, in consideration of the sum of £2,700, to Sir Walter Pye and William Scudamore of Ballingham.

In all probability, Treville Park was at least as thickly populated in 1605 as is the present Whitfield estate and its immediate environs. The Park Farm, James Quarrell's farm, John Quarrell's house at Weetewood (Whitewood) at the eastern edge of the Park near the hamlet of Didley, and the original Whitfield, were merely some of the more obvious dwellings. Evidence was given in 1610 that within comparatively recent times there had been as many as thirty houses within the bounds. The abode of William Morgan, therefore, whether Whitfield or not, may well have been little more elevated socially than that of William Walker of The Darren, and the choice of Whitfield for the celebration of mass as little significant. It should not be forgotten, however, that the ecclesiastical uncertainty surrounding Treville may have been a factor favouring Catholic activity there, in fashion parallel with the loneliness of the middle Monnow valley. The social status and numbers of the population in Treville Park in 1605 may also provide one determinant in the consideration of the identity of William Morgan which must follow.

Cadwallader's parish, from Wormbridge to Allensmore, was

kept in close relation with Catholics in Hereford The chief means
of liaison was provided by Rice Griffiths, an apparent conformist.
Commended to the Bishop by Richard Bancroft, Archbishop of
Canterbury, as a one-time priest who had seen the error of his
ways and who would be useful in seducing other Catholics from
their allegiance to the Pope, he used his access to the Bishop to
give prior warning to his co-religionaries of any action intended
against them. He often met Cadwallader secretly to pass on the
latest news and provide him with books. When the Bishop on two
occasions commanded the seizure of Cadwallader, Griffiths sent
him immediate word, the second time by one William Simonds
in the following terms: 'Commend me to Mr. Rogers[14] and bid
him looke to himselfe and let him not come neere Arxton nor
Sugwas.' That he should keep away from his father's house was
obvious advice enough: it would perhaps be unwise to attempt
from this message to prove too conclusively that he was, at more
propitious moments, a visitor or even a minister to Sir Charles
Morgan's household also.

There were many other instances of Griffiths's doubleness. He
had continued not only to associate with Cadwallader and
Edwards but to exercise his own priestly functions. He and
Edwards were alleged to have been at the house of Mrs. Elizabeth
Morgan, a widow, in Eaton Bishop about Easter 1605. According
to one witness, he heard confessions only: according to another, he
said mass. He himself at his examination admitted saying mass but
denied consecrating. But such fine distinctions were probably lost
on those who sought his blood. William Price, parson of Eaton,
roundly declared that he had been responsible for the enticement
of some forty parishioners into the Catholic faith, which, if true,
would suggest that his ministrations on the south bank of Wye
had been both forceful and regular. Temporarily, at any rate, his
running with the hare and hunting with the hounds had proved
more than profitable.

Within earshot, too, was another Catholic of dubious record
and equivocal behaviour in the person of John Smith of Kilpeck, a

layman. According to Paul Delahay, who sent the information to
the Earl of Salisbury in October 1605, Smith had betrayed a priest
named Silvester to the authorities in 1588, but since that time had
re-established himself among his fellows and was known as a
dangerous recusant. Together with William Morgan and Eaton,
alias North, the seminary priest, he was alleged to have tried to
create disaffection at the time of the King's accession. Who this
John Smith was has not been established from any pedigree so far
examined, but he was a brother-in-law of that John James of
Kilpeck who collected the tithes of Treville up to 1613, and
wealthy enough to give his sister Elizabeth 'threescore pounds of
lawfull money of England' on the occasion of her marriage.
Resident at Milbrooke, presumably in the parish of Kilpeck, he
was styled 'yeoman', but had either the experience or the wit to
sign his own name, an achievement beyond the powers either of
Thomas Morgan of Arkston or of John Philipps of Kivernoll,
both of whom essayed the rank of 'gent'.[15] If he was an incomer to
the district, as seems possible, and one with experience of London
and the counsels of the great, he may have been driven by
jealousy of the dominant position achieved by Rice Griffiths in the
esteem of local Catholics to betray his trust a second time. Griffiths
had commonly informed Smith, possibly because of his superior
understanding, of the contents of all letters passing between the
Bishop of Hereford and Sir Charles Morgan of Arkston: at length,
however, provoked by Griffiths's self-importance (and, as he
afterwards insisted, by his 'lewdness'), Smith first told Sir Charles
(whose own position then became peculiarly difficult) and later
made his defection irrevocable by sending William Parry to
inform the Bishop himself of Griffiths's treachery. This happened
about October 1604.[16] The Bishop made no immediate and overt
move against Griffiths or his fellow-Catholics, but knowledge of
the disclosure and fear of its consequences may well have been the
basis of William Morgan's assertion under duress that he and his
fellow-rebels moved first 'because the Bishop meant to take some
hard course' with them. As for John Smith, his was a part cast in

shadow: during the commotion of June 1605 he was apparently already a prisoner in the Gatehouse. That this was a result of some counter-accusation against him is made less likely by the fact that William Morgan wrote to him in prison during the period of riot, hardly a time for a message of vilification. Nevertheless, when released, he was once again to act in a manner which earned the opprobrium of most of his fellow-Catholics.

What had been in the balance in the autumn of 1604, it would appear, was a conflict either of policy or personal prestige between Rice Griffiths and John Smith. There is simply not enough evidence to show how this was related, if at all, to any rival groupings among Herefordshire recusants.

Smith's intervention certainly diminished the powers of Rice Griffiths in the diocese of Hereford, but the latter's arrest, when it finally came, was fraught with greater difficulties for the Bishop than had been his freedom. While at large he had nullified the Bishop's intentions against the recusants: in custody, he was the cause of an open breach between the Bishop and the Archbishop of Canterbury, whose irritable self-esteem was endangered by the arrest. It must be borne in mind, however, that Archbishop Bancroft had already taken offence before this issue arose. Ever since the book of canons compiled in Convocation under his chairmanship in March 1604 had been attacked in the Commons and a Bill carried to the effect that no canon passed in the last ten years should be capable of hurt to the life, liberty or lands of any person unless it should be confirmed by the House, he had been bitterly antagonistic to the authority of the legislature and the civil courts. His *Articuli Cleri*, which he was to lay before the Privy Council in Michaelmas 1605, were a prolonged attempt, with the backing of the Crown, to repudiate the 'prohibitions' which the civil judges laid against the proceedings of ecclesiastical courts and to free those ecclesiastical courts from the interference of the law. One move in this campaign of his was certainly the letter he wrote to all his suffragans on March 12, 1605, underlining the canons to be observed in dealing with recusancy and pointing

out that bishops were *ex officio* justices of the peace and as such
should exercise their civil functions with more diligence. They
should also certify the details of known recusants to the Archbishop with all convenient speed. Here, then, was the head and
front of Bishop Bennett's offending. He had certified the riot to
the Privy Council.

It may be felt that the Bishop of Hereford's action was natural-
ness itself, since the outbreak was one of serious violence and
plainly a police matter. But Bancroft chose to regard it as disobedience.

On top of this came the arrest of Rice Griffiths, again by the
Bishop and not by secular authority. Another favourite gambit
jeopardized, and by an underling. It was hardly in Bancroft to be
pleased. For at least four years before this he had been busily
playing upon the differences between the secular clergy of the
Catholic Church and the Jesuits, with a view to the enticement of
the former into the Anglican fold. In July 1601 he was negotiating
with Sir Robert Cecil for a safe-conduct for Bagshaw and Bluett,
two of the main actors in the Wisbech Stirs and since that time
notorious opponents of the Jesuits. In August of the same year he
was attempting to use the ill-fated William Watson against the
Society. He had busied himself throughout in studying the litera-
ture illustrating the points of difference between the two Catholic
wings, and had earned suspicious glances at the Hampton Court
Conference on this account. That section of the Conference to
which *all* Catholics were traitors would have been able to exchange
suspicion for fierce invective had they known of the man-to-man
tone adopted by Bluett to Bancroft in September 1601 when he
was still Bishop of London, 'considering', as he wrote, 'in what
terms our business standeth'. But the Earl of Salisbury was not a
colleague for such choice revelations: the details of the Bishop's
negotiations never came out.

The undersized firstfruits of Bancroft's policy of *division* had
appeared early in 1603 when he had received the proffered allegiance of fifteen seminary priests, brought by four of their

number. Anathema to the Puritan interest, he was always ready to interview and pardon abjured priests. Rice Griffiths was such an one. A Cornish priest named Penkevell who had been in the Marshalsea was another. Wherever a Catholic might be won, the Archbishop put on his most tolerant countenance. Sir Tobie Mathew, returning to England in 1606 as a declared Catholic and paying suit at Lambeth, reported that Bancroft embraced him and looked as kindly upon him 'as that face could tell how to do'.

Now the Bishop of Hereford's action made public the allegation that Griffiths had fooled Bancroft to the top of his bent. The Archbishop had no doubt imagined that the careful placing of contacts such as this seemingly relapsed priest would enable him to control the Catholic population even in strongly recusant areas. No doubt the dissemination of information among his fellows, information emanating from an inspired source in London, was the semi-official purpose of Rice Griffiths's attachment to Hereford. For the Bishop, therefore, to appear to be sapient where his master had been a gull would hardly breed more health in the episcopal palace. On the contrary. The Archbishop was thoroughly exasperated. For his part, Bennett had turned obstinate. He had no favour to lose, or preferment. As well stand to it.

There is a hint too that in the case of Rice Griffiths the Archbishop had some private reason for being touchy. It may have been merely that Griffiths was not overstating the case in impressing upon the Catholic bucolics of Herefordshire that he had 'absolute intelligence in State matters' and was 'greate with the Lo: Byshoppe of Cant'.[17] On the other hand, the reason may have been even less worthy, though its nature cannot be determined.[18] Whatever lay behind the innuendoes, it was made plain that the Archbishop 'takes it offensively'. Bennett now had to face sedulous misinterpretation and enmity in high places. His prospects of a personal success had become minute.

Unhappily perched in a similar, though not identical, cleft stick were the magistrates expected to assist the Bishop in executing the

Council's policy against the Catholics. The majority were of no assistance whatsoever. They had their own problems.

First in equivocation, if not in eminence, must come Sir Charles Morgan of Arkston,[19] to whom reference has already been made. A descendant of that David ap Gwilym ap Morgan of Llanddewi Ysgyrid under the lee of the Black Mountains, who in the early years of the sixteenth century had come down to the lower slopes to marry Anne Delahay, the heiress of Arkston, Charles Morgan had succeeded to his patrimony in 1602[20] and ever since had hovered uneasily between the Catholic tradition of his forebears, still exemplified by his mother, the sister of William and Ambrose Griffiths, his uncle (or great-uncle) Thomas Morgan of Blackmoor, his younger brothers Thomas and Edward, who lived at Arkston with him, and his brother-in-law Rice ap Rice of Kilpeck,[21] on the one hand, and, on the other, the new and searching demands both of magistracy and of legal and social requirement within the county. Arkston had once had its own private chapel, and the will of old David ap Gwilym ap Morgan in 1523 had made provision both for a priest to say daily mass at the altar of St. Stephen there and for a chamber for that priest's residence. To what extent the family devotion had been weakened by evil times it is impossible to say, but if Roger Cadwallader occasionally said mass at Arkston, Charles Morgan, now Sir Charles, took good care that he personally could not be proved to be cognizant of it. Lord of the manor of Treville and one of the few magistrates in southwest Herefordshire, he found it awkward enough to have to answer for the recusancy of his family and of many of his tenants. If justification for his caution were required, he could probably assert that their relative freedom of worship depended with some exactitude upon his personal sacrifice in accepting office and playing watchdog for the Bishop. Further than that he could hardly go without conviction, and conviction he did not possess. He had, however, lent his weight in 1602 to the attempt of the Baskervilles to recover their sequestered lands and at Elizabeth's death had been solicited to take up arms in the Catholic interest. But he was not really a likely man for such heroics: he had continued, instead, to pay lip-service to the Bishop's authority and had carefully gone through the motions of laying a recusant by the heels when so commanded. For him, then, the outbreak of June 1605 was a crisis of spirit as well as of activity. He attempted to evade the issue by innocently leaving the county for London the day after the trouble began, but for his pains was committed to the Fleet for neglect of duty.[22]

Another in much the same case was Sir Roger Bodenham of Rotherwas, on the Wye a few miles south-east of Hereford, 'a delicious seat', according to the antiquarian Thomas Blount of Orleton some decades later, 'where there is a fair parlour full of coats of arms'. His wife, the Lady Bridget, a daughter of Sir Humphrey Baskerville of Eardisley, whose considerable lands, up river near the Breconshire border, had since 1589 been subject to the legal depredations of wardship, was described by the Bishop of Hereford as 'an imperious dame of high stomach and stirring humour, who countenances all priests and recusants'. Sir Roger himself, a Papist of more discretion and allied by marriage to the Morgans of Machen and Tredegar,[23] had been suspected of following, albeit at a distance, the too-faithful courses of the Earl of Essex's steward, Sir Gelly Meyrick, who preceded his master to execution. A Deputy-Lieutenant of the Shire and a Knight of the Bath, he had a greater degree of political experience and certainly more nerve than Sir Charles Morgan, although his knighthood was no older. Untrusted by the Bishop, he played his double game skilfully to the end. Both he and Sir Charles had been dubbed after James's accession, during the first disposition of an afterwards increasingly tortuous policy. Herefordshire had to pay for these mistakes.

Men of similar type among the magistrates were Anthony Pembridge of Wellington, who had been elected for the Borough of Hereford to the Parliament of 1597, though, oddly enough, in opposition to the nominee of the Earl of Essex, and Roger Mynors of Treiago, St. Weonards. Pembridge's wife was an indicted recusant. Mynors, scion of a family long-established in southern Herefordshire and well endowed with lands, some of which we:e to be found as far west and north of Treiago as the parishes of Kilpeck and Kentchurch, was descended on his mother's side from the Vaughans of Porthamal near Talgarth. Outwardly his position looked secure enough; himself Steward of the Crown Manor of Garway, he had a younger brother, Henry, who had acquired, probably by purchase, the court office of Sergeant of the Carriages. But behind this façade there was much equivocation: Roger's wife, once Jane Harley of the Harleys of Brampton Bryan, was an indicted recusant and representative of the older tradition of her family. It is perhaps, significant only of the relatively late incursion into the Marches of the extremes of religious controversy that she should have had for nephew the determined Puritan protagonist Sir Robert Harley. Roger's brother William, next in age to himself, was deeply involved in the disturbances in the Monnow valley in this summer of 1605, and if William Mynors of Oldfield in Garway, named by William Morgan as one of his lieutenants, should prove not to have been identical with William Mynors of Treiago, the relationship cannot be wrong by more than a generation. It is always possible, too, though by no means proven, that Jane Mynors may have been sister to Dr. Harley, the lawyer-physician of Hereford. The Treiago family stood, willingly or not, on the edge of conspiracy. The Bishop was possibly not guilty of grave exaggeration in describing the participation of such persons in the work of justice at a time of riot as 'very pernicious to our lives'.

On the other hand, while the ramifications of recusancy among the gentlemen of the shire fully justified the repetitive tones of episcopal alarm, there were some justices at least who were ready to carry out their orders against the Papists. First among these was undoubtedly Sir James Scudamore of Holme Lacy, downstream from Rotherwas, whose heraldic achievement quartered the paternal coat of Scudamore, 'gules, three stirrups leathered and buckled or'. His father, Sir John of Holme Lacy, still alive and full of years,[24] had been M.P. for Herefordshire in five parliaments, gentleman usher to Queen Elizabeth, friend of Sir Thomas Bodley and benefactor of his library, and, with a more local generosity, the procurer 'of the goodly Bridge neere unto Rosse, over the River Wye'. Sir James, the son, 'famous and fortunate in his time', had been knighted before Cadiz in 1596 and subsequently held up to the mirror of chivalry as Sir Scudamour in Spenser's *Faerie Queene*.[25] Becoming M.P. for Herefordshire in 1604, he had apparently rid himself of the unpopular odour of association with the Earl of Essex. 'Of the rest', wrote the Bishop of Hereford, 'I find Sir James Scudamore to be most ready and faithful in the service, and stands closely unto me.' Although he was as vulnerable in his relatives as Bodenham or Morgan, having indeed for cousin the redoubtable Lady Bridget, a Scudamore by her mother, and for nephew Father David Baker, who in 1607 was to refound the Benedictine Order in Britain, nothing has been discovered to place that verdict on Sir James in doubt.

Two other magistrates, apparently somewhat removed geographically from the storm centre, had better reasons for supporting the Bishop than are immediately evident. William Rudhall of Rudhall between Ross and Brampton Abbotts had married his daughter Joyce to Sir Samuel Aubrey, a collateral of the Aubreys of Llantrithid, Glamorgan, who lived at Clehonger, south of Wye and hard by Madley and Eaton Bishop, and in 1602 another daughter, Joan, to Walter Pye of The Mynde, a mere two miles south-east of Treville. His interest in the immediate region of riot was also perhaps more acute because of a sixty-year lease of the manor of Llangua, between Wormbridge and Grosmont, which he had obtained from Thomas Scudamore of Kentchurch in 1593. There was undoubtedly an extensive cousinship between the Rudhalls and equivocators like the Mynors and Baskerville families, but William's wife was a cousin of Sir Herbert Croft and his closest links were with the cautious and well-informed household of The Mynde. Thomas Kyrle of Walford and Eaton Tregoes,[26] an ancestor of 'The Man of Ross', was Walter Pye's maternal grandfather. In both cases, therefore, there was a reason for their reliability to which a chronicler ignorant either of their religious attitude or their personal quality may give at least some weight.

Most interesting of the meagre group on whom the Bishop could rely, however, was Rowland Vaughan of Whitehouse in the Golden Valley, at no great distance north-westwards from the disaffected area. Cousin to his namesake of Porthamal, Talgarth, Rowland was the second son of Watkin Vaughan of Bredwardine and grand-nephew to Blanche Parry, Queen Elizabeth's 'great friend and Bedchamber woman'. After a few years at Court under the 'carefull though crabbed austerity' of his grand-aunt, and a few more in the Irish Wars acquiring 'the country-disease' he had returned to Herefordshire, yielding to the blandishments of his kinswoman Anne Powell[27] and obtaining Whitehouse in Vow-church[28] and a dominating wife for his pains. More and more the reminiscent bachelor, he betook himself in the end to empirical attempts to improve his estates, producing in 1610 a remarkable book on *Waterworks*,[29] probably the least informative and most amusing volume on such a subject ever written. It contains a wealth of complaint and vituperative aside, together with a fine athletic taste for rambling. There can be little doubt that neither Rowland nor his drainages were a great success. The ex-metropolitan with the upright carriage, whom Queen Elizabeth had once noticed at a shoot in Islington Fields and declared 'a feat man to attend her service', was becoming soured and incoherent, more impressive in ruin than when architecturally complete. The 'watry workemanshipp' of his Stanke Royal was many times lost in 'a hotch-potch of speach'.

What little can be learned about his leanings, religious and political, suggests that he drew heavily on his early experience and looked Courtwards for a lead. In 1597 he was certainly seeking to cultivate the Cecil connection. One of his near relatives by marriage was Sir Robert Knollys, whose mother, Katherine Carey, had been first cousin to Qeeen Elizabeth, and while such a relationship may have been of little or no material advantage to him, it is scarcely possible to suppose that he did not at times hear from the anterooms of Court what puff King James had given the wind some few travelling days past. In 1605, in any case, his son John had been entered as a student of the Inner Temple, and there is every likelihood that, with a father's anxiety, he had by this time taken up the lodging near St. Dunstan's Church in Fleet Street of which he was to make use for the next twenty years. Rowland's own claim for himself was that he was 'no Papist, nor Puritan, but a true Protestant according to the King's injunctions'. If he achieved this as a matter of sincere belief, doubting neither the King's intentions nor the permanency of his injunctions, then his religious convictions ran remarkably in harness with a well-informed political calculation. His tone was often very critical of the local clergy, but a deal of this was wisdom after the event, shadow-fighting under patronage. Of what value his service was to the Bishop does not appear. At least he came when sent for.

One other lay figure, apparently not a justice, must be mentioned. The Bishop, as a result of the offence taken at his hands by the Archbishop of Canterbury, deliberately called in Paul Delahay of Allt-yr-ynys in Walterstone parish, five or six miles south-west of Treville and across the county boundary, to sit with him in examination of prisoners and witnesses. The point of this manoeuvre is not far to seek. Delahay, described by Bishop Mathew (for reasons which do not suffice) as 'an adventurer' who 'had preyed upon old Lord Burghley's love of pedigree', was the husband of Jane, daughter or granddaughter[30] of William Cecil, first or 'cosen germaine' to Burghley and until his death in 1598 'possessed of the foresaid howse of Halterennes in Ewias land'. Doubts have been cast from time to time upon the validity of the connection between the Court Cecils and the unimpressive farmhouse in Walterstone parish, and there has been no serious belief in Cecil influence or interest in Monmouthshire. Bishop Mathew, for instance, has allowed both this and sympathy with John Arnold and the Essex following, to colour his entire attitude to Paul

Delahay. Yet there is no real room for argument, as a careful
scrutiny of the Salisbury Papers shows. Delahay, though not as yet
identifiable from pedigree, was not a stranger to the district: there
were Delahays at Arkston before the Morgans came, and the name
is common enough in deeds of the fourteenth and fifteenth century among the Kentchurch Court Papers. It is not disputed that
William Cecil had by his will disinherited his own eight daughters
and made over all his lands to his cousin Burghley, to keep the
name of Cecil green in Ewyas land. Paul Delahay, husband of one
of the disinherited daughters, was in 1605 certainly a tenant of the
Earl of Salisbury, and probably his steward. It can be established,
independent of Cecil legend or Delahay propaganda, that Salisbury stood possessed of lands in the vicinity in 1602[31] and that his
family were still the chief landowners thereabouts as late as 1652.

It is difficult to see what Bishop Bennett intended by Delahay's
certification of his actions if not the increase of his credit with the
Earl of Salisbury as an offset to Archbishop Bancroft's displeasure.
That party in the Council which was out of sympathy with the
unnecessary delicacy of seeking to separate one Catholic from
another may have looked to Salisbury for approval, if only because, now that Essex was gone, there was nowhere else to look.
Yet the identification of personal and group attitudes within the
Council suffers sadly from want of evidence. Essex, it is true, had
for his own political advantage called Cecil 'Spanish',[32] and the
relations of 'the little beagle' with Richard Bancroft, both as
Bishop of London and subsequently as Archbishop, were as jovial
and familiar (on paper) as either the contained spirit or the grim
visage could ensure. But Bishop Bennett, we must suppose, was
in dire straits. Whether or not he turned with reason to the Earl of
Salisbury, from whom else could he hope for an offset to the
archiepiscopal rage?

Delahay, then, was the instrument to hand. That the tenant of
Allt-yr-ynys had been a man who made the most of his Cecil connection may easily be established:[33] but where Court favour was in
point who save a few would not have fallen by this stricture? The

confident tone of his request to Cecil in 1600 for a wardship, and Sir Herbert Croft's preparedness in the same year to believe that 'Paul Delahay hath done some wrong by possessing Mr. Secretary with an opinion' both indicate an established relationship between the two. Almost certainly Delahay was from 1598 onwards executor and steward of the Cecil lands both at Allt-yr-ynys and nearby and looked upon himself not only as the guardian of Cecil prestige locally,[34] but also as a protagonist of sorts in the political lists. Whatever his importunity or presumption he escaped the comment reserved for those who *did* prey on the Cecil pedigree.[35] If this connection was a straw, as Bishop Mathew would have it, then the Bishop of Hereford, on his own showing, was like to drown. It is reasonable, however, to suppose that Dr. Bennett knew what he was about, and that when Delahay wrote that the Bishop's 'service and his forwardness against recusants has been the occasion of the reformation of many in these parts' he was doing something of actual value to the Bishop's cause. If not, he was meddling in a manner particularly disastrous to 'adventurers'.

The interposition of Delahay, nevertheless, came too late in the day to cover the essential weakness of the Bishop's position. The previous March, before the outbreak, he had been pleading for an ecclesiastical commission against the recusants in his diocese. Earlier still, in 1604, his certification of sixty recusants as attending mass had been entirely frustrated by an *a certiorari* which removed the charge to the King's Bench and there killed it. 'Without special assistance from your Honours' he wrote to the Council on June 1, 1605, he had no hopes of making his power effective. Had he known then that both he and the magistrates were to serve a further term as the whipping boys of royal policy, his language might have been even more desperate. Confronted with the hostility of the Archbishop, denied any additional power by the Council, assisted nominally by magistrates affected by sympathy with the recusants, and required to persist in a policy which he regarded as having fostered the outbreak in the first place, Dr. Bennett's prospects were as bleak as the onset of winter. Those of

D

faithful members of the magistracy, such as Sir James Scudamore, were very little brighter. Being on the spot was a fact and inescapable.

NOTES

[1] 'Mr. Morgan the younger of Lanternham, with whom the said Jones the Jesuit is now ofte, sometymes for a month togither.' *S.P.* 14, Vol. XIV, 40.

[2] Caraman's *John Gerard* (p. 255), presumably following Foley, op. cit., VII, Pt. I, p. 553, makes the suggestion that Robert Jones and Robert North were identical. The Sheriff's List of 1604, however (*S.P.* 14, Vol. XIV, 40), makes it clear that Jones, alias Holland, the Jesuit, and Eaton, alias North, the seminary priest, were quite different people, although the latter was Jones's immediate instrument. The incident quoted by Caraman (p. 202) of North in Worcester Gaol in 1606 does not suggest Jones either in spirit or locale. Foley's argument depends mainly upon an assertion that three letters, all dated in October 1606, and directed 'against the oath-takers' (i.e. Thomas Wright, alias Carpenter, and his followers who judged it lawful to attend Protestant sermons) were from the same hand. The first two, signed Robert Angelinus and Robert Draper, were subsequently attributed to Robert Jones: the third was signed Robert North. It appears just as likely that Robert Eaton, alias North, was the author of all three, albeit under instruction. Foley's index, in any case, was in this instance at fault. In Vol. VII, Pt. I, p. 218 he quoted a description of Reginald Eaton as given by Robert Weston, a spy, in 1591: 'a litle shorte felowe, a broad flaxey bearde, some 34 or 35 yeares olde.' He became a Jesuit in 1609/10 and, although a native of Lincolnshire, was associated during most of his working life with the College of St. Francis Xavier (Wales).

[3] Born 1563 in the diocese of St. Asaph, he joined the Society in 1587, after studying at Douai. He was at Cologne in 1597, and very little is known of his work in his native land. He appears to have died before 1610.

[4] During the hard winter of 1946–7 subsidence in a field near The Cwm was unmistakably caused by the collapse of a passage leading in the direction of a smaller house now known as Nunnery Cottage.

[5] On the land of Mr. Brown of Darren Cottage is an extensive site, apparently provided with dams and fishponds (and on which a man and a horse are reputedly buried in a common grave) about which there appears to be no certain local knowledge. It finds no mention on the parish map in Skenfrith Church (*tempo* Henry VIII). Since, however, Mr. Brown's land is charged with a condition that 14*s*. o*d*. per annum must be paid by the lessee towards the upkeep of the chancel of the Church of the Hospitallers at Garway, long since in ruins and only recently rediscovered, the connections of this site seem fairly obvious.

[6] A facsimile of the Map of the Manor of Syneffraid Henry VIII, on the wall

of Skenfrith Church. The original is in the British Museum. It is true that the Darren Wood and the farther side of Monnow are not within the manor limits, but a number of holdings outside those limits are indicated and it is a reasonable presumption that if The Darren were a house of importance, it would have been marked on this map.

⁷ MS. No. 2464, Garway. The Darrein, Hasell Feild and other Lands Admeasured for George Lewis Gent. by Tho. Croft. 1698. The total acreage then of The Darren was just over 15. Hazelfield was a distance eastward and higher up the hill. It is now in ruins and difficult of access.

⁸ Tierney's Dodd, op. cit., Vol. IV, p. 179. The other two seculars who suffered were George Nappier (at Oxford, on November 9) and Thomas Somers, alias Wilson (at Tyburn, on December 10). John Roberts, O.S.B., martyred at Tyburn on the same day as Somers, was the only regular.

⁹ *Cal. of Salis. MSS.*, Part XII, pp. 631–2. The Bishop of London to Sir Robert Cecil, Feb. 1, 1602–3. The Bishop reported that 'Mr. Benet and Mr. Watson are much moved with their presumption in not resting themselves upon Her Majesty's clemency'. The four who appeared personally were Robert Charnocke, Anthony Hebborne, Francis Barnbye and Thomas Bluett, the last-named being the 'factious priest' who laid a deposition against William Weston, the Jesuit, at Wisbech, accusing him of subordination to the Infanta of Spain. *William Weston*, trans. Caraman, pp. 196–7.

¹⁰ The Bishop of Hereford wrote on June 22, 1605 that 'it is . . . insinuated that Cadwallador, the priest . . . had (his) finger in the late Watson's intended treason'. *S.P.* 14, Vol. XIV, 52.

¹¹ Exchequer (KR) *Depositions* (E.134) 8 Jas. I Hil. 9. The Commissioners were James Price Parry, gent., Thomas Morrice, clerk, John Philipps and Hugh Russell, gentlemen. They heard the evidence in the Market Hall at Grosmont on August 29, 1610.

¹² Ibid. Deposition of Richard Sayer of Little Birch, yeoman. I am indebted to Lady Mary Clive for the suggestion that 'Park Hall in the Township of Trivell' which Sayer gave as the site of the chapel, was Park Orles, a patch of woodland in Treville park.

¹³ With the exception of lands granted to Charles Rogers of Monkhall in 1613.

¹⁴ Cadwallader's name in the field.

¹⁵ Hereford City Library, Pilley Collection, Drawer 2, No. 8.

¹⁶ *Examinacons Rice Griffiths*, Hatfield MSS. Parry delivered his message to the Bishop 'some ten moneths paste'.

¹⁷ William Morgan, in custody, thought of him as 'one Griffith that was with my Lo: of Canterbury'. Examination of Wm. Morgan. *S.P.* 14, Vol. XIV, 45.

¹⁸ John Smith (Hatfield MSS.) deposed that 'Rice Griffiths tould him in Lent laste that he would be revenged on one Sir Edmund Ashfielde for callinge him a lewed priest. He sayd he would preserve it for a tricke to stoppe the Byshop of Cant. mouthe if ever he came into any question'. There is also evidence that William Morgan, chief actor in the disturbance, claimed to be a kinsman to the

Archbishop and wrote to Smith to tell 'one Griffith that was with my Lo: to satisfie him, last the connstable would aggravate the matter'. Examination of Wm. Morgan, ibid.

[19] Prof. A. H. Dodd, in his article 'Wales and the Scottish Succession', (Trans. Cymmrodorion, 1937) is mistaken in identifying this man with Sir Charles Morgan of Pencarn, Glamorgan. The latter was far too young in 1605 and would be difficult to explain, in any case, as a J.P. in Herefordshire. He went abroad and remained there, spending many years as Governor of Bergen and marrying a Dutch wife. There is no evidence at all that he was ever in the Treville district.

[20] Thomas Morgan of Arkston, his father, was alive in 1601 (G. T. Clark, op. cit., p. 258) but seems to have died in the year following.

[21] According to the Bishop of Hereford's letter of June 22, 1605 (*S.P.* 14, Vol. XIV, 52). There is plenty of evidence for Rice ap Rice's recusancy and participation in the troubles of these weeks but none from pedigrees that Sir Charles Morgan ever had a brother-in-law of this name.

[22] G.D. to Sir Everard Digby, June 11, 1605. *Cal. of Salis. MSS.*, Pt. XVII, p. 252. His endorsement of the Bishop of Hereford's letter of June 1, however, casts doubt on the promptitude of his departure. *Cal. of Salis. MSS.*, Pt. XVII, p.235. More probably his committal was the result of the arrival in Hereford-shire of Sir Herbert Croft, since the two were old enemies. Indeed, Sir Charles's dispatch to London, of which this is the only mention, may be the best confir-mation that Croft did, in fact, come down.

[23] His sister Elizabeth was the widow of Sir Thomas Morgan 'the Warrior' and his daughter of the same name married Sir Thomas Morgan of Machen, M.P. for Monmouthshire 1588–9 and Sheriff of the County in 1581.

[24] He died April 14, 1623.

[25] Book IV. Also in Higford's *Institutions of a Gentleman*, where a description is given of his tilting before Queen Elizabeth.

[26] John Hobson Matthews in Trans. Catholic Record Society, Vol. II, p. 289. Dodd's *Church History*, Vol. IV, p. 100, gives 'Mr. Reole', but no such person appears anywhere else, and Kyrle is plainly right.

[27] She was the daughter of Griffith ap Howell and Jane Parry, daughter of Simon Parry of Whitehouse and niece both to Miles Parry of New Court and Blanche Parry, Queen Elizabeth's 'bedchamber woman'. Since Rowland him-self was the son of Joan Parry of New Court, daughter to Miles, Anne, his wife, was by birth his second cousin. This identification conflicts entirely with that given both by Ellen Beatrice Wood in *Rowland Vaughan his Booke* (London, 1897) pp. x–xi, who asserts that Rowland's wife was Elizabeth Vaughan, daughter of Rowland Vaughan of Porthamal and Elizabeth Parry of New Court (and therefore his *first* cousin) and by C. A. Bradford, *Rowland Vaughan* (London, 1937), pp. 3–4 (citing Theophilus Jones, *History of Brecknockshire* Vol. III, p. 43), who identifies her with Elizabeth Parry of New Court (referred to above), who was Rowland's aunt. The assertion that Rowland's wife was Anne Powell is based on two grounds: (i) The pedigree in *Llyfr Baglan*, (p. 44) easily

the most reliable of those available, (ii) The fact that Rowland was resident at Whitehouse in April 1607 (*Kentchurch Court Papers* Vol. I, No. 1882), 1609 and 1614. His crest and initials, with the date 1613, are to be found fixed to the upper part of the roof posts in the parish church of Vowchurch (Trans. Woolhope Club 1914–17, p. 94). In 1623 he described himself as 'late of White House'. (Bradford, op. cit., p. 6).

²⁸ Rowland's mother, Joan Parry, had been co-heiress with her sister Elizabeth of the New Court property. It seems reasonable to suppose that Rowland lived at New Court until his marriage.

²⁹ The full title is as follows: *Most Approved and Long Experienced Waterworkes Containing the manure of winter and summer draining of meadow and pasture by the advantage of the least rivers, brooke, fount, or waterprille adjacent, thereby to make those grounds (especially if they be drye) more fertile ten for one. Also a demonstration of a project for the great benefit of the Commonwealth generally, but of Herefordshire especially.* By Rowland Vaughan, Esq., London, 1610. Amusing too is the project he entered upon to stimulate sales. Most of the extant copies have on the flyleaf a promise from the author to pay at a future date the sum of £2 to the possessor of a copy of the book. Whether this ruinous promise was ever honoured does not appear.

³⁰ Trans. Woolhope Club, 1906, p. 260, gives Delahay as son-in-law to William Cecil of Allt-yr-ynys. According to Francis Thin the herald, however, (Cymmrodorion Record Series, No. 4, *A Catalogue of MSS. Relating to Wales in the British Museum,* Part 1, pp. 67–70, Lansdowne Collection 104(*b*) f. 183), he married Jane, granddaughter of William Cecil. The discrepancy is, perhaps, not important, save that in the latter case William Cecil must have survived till all his daughters had married and gone away, leaving Paul Delahay, the husband of a granddaughter, as the most convenient executor.

³¹ *Cal. of Salis. MSS.,* Pt. XII., Sept. 17, 1602. A letter from Nicholas Fortescue to Robert Cecil offered to arrange the passage of lands at Michaelchurch into his possession. These lands were 'within a very little mile of Halterennes', which was clearly, from the letter, Cecil's property. Trans. Woolhope Club, 1906, pp. 257–9, (notes by Herbert Jones, Esq., of Ewyas Harold), states that a survey of Allt-yr-ynys, both house and grounds, was made in 1647 and that in the windows were the arms of Cecil and Delahay, in painted glass.

³² Referred to by Cecil himself in Nov. 1602. *Cal. of Salis. MSS.,* Part XIV, p. 237.

³³ E.g. *Cal. of Salis. MSS.,* Pt. X., p. 97, where Delahay makes some play with the family seat of the Cecils in church and its violation during divine service by his enemies. To the same class may belong his letter of June 23, 1598 explaining the decay (unimportance?) of Allt-yr-ynys. Trans. Woolhope Club, 1906, p. 260.

³⁴ William Cecil was in a position to ask favours of Sir Robert Cecil in April 1597 (*vide* Bradford, op. cit., p. 5, letter dated April 30 on behalf of Rowland Vaughan). After his demise in 1598 and the transfer of his property

to the Secretary of State, Delahay wrote to Cecil to the effect that 'to the credit
of the house of Alterinis' he had let it be understood that the funeral expenses
had been paid (to the extent of £100) by Sir Robert. In all probability they were
paid by the estate and not by the legatee. Trans. Woolhope Club, 1906, p. 260.

³⁵ A letter from one William George (*Cal. of Salis. MSS.*, Pt. XVII, p. 595,
dated 1605) claiming to have been thrown into prison as a victim of the Cecil-
Arnold feud (on which Delahay also had much to say) and going on to expatiate
on his attempts to incorporate Bleddyn's coat impaled in the Cecil 'pedigree out
of Wales', is superscribed by Sir Robert: 'I desire none of these vain toys, nor
to hear of such absurdities.'

CHAPTER IV

Ambush and Armed Mass

BY the beginning of June 1605 both the rebels and the local hierarchy were nonplussed, the former to explain away what they had done, the latter what they had omitted to do. Of these situations that of the Bishop of Hereford and the magistrates was superficially the easier to remedy. They had only by 'dexterous means' to seize William Morgan of Treville Park.

At or after midnight on the eve of Corpus Christi (June 4 or 5) the Bishop, accompanied by Sir James Scudamore and Sir Roger Bodenham, arrived at Morgan's house, whether that were Whitfield or The Parke. There was nothing very dexterous about this, and it is not surprising to learn that Morgan and his friends, served by sundry runners and intelligencers, had made adequate preparations. Near the house were disposed upwards of sixty men, perhaps as many as a hundred, armed with bows, pikes, bills, swords and javelins, some twenty or thirty of them in a vallett[1] or wooded dell called The Cockett[2] (perhaps identifiable with the present Cockyard Wood) and rather more in another vallett near Morgan's house. These dispositions suggest that the Bishop and his party were expected to leave Treville Park for Kingstone or Arkston, and not by the more easterly path towards Didley and Winnall. What was planned was not a direct attack on the Bishop's party as it approached Morgan's house. The violence, when it came, was to be provoked by high-handed arrest, and its perpetrators, or such of them as were sufficiently knowledgeable, had one eye on future excuse even while the weapons lay cold under their hands.

In a word, Morgan was to be rescued as soon as taken. The ambush had been ready since about eleven o'clock, ever since the runners had first brought news that the Bishop had left Hereford: one Morrice, a preacher and perhaps a counter-enthusiast, who happened upon some of the recusants as they lay in wait, got from them no explanation beyond the cryptic phrase that 'they were watching for a good hour'.

Among these desperadoes were the unyielding participants in the earlier scenes of violence, James Coles and William Chadnor, the weavers of Hungerstone, Leonard Marsh of Kingstone, the prisoner rescued from the High Constable of the Hundred ten days before, and William Caunt of Madley. In their company were other, newer figures: Thomas Price of Madley, massing clerk to Rice Griffiths and an active proselytizer, Henry Williams of Dore[3] and his son George, Thomas John Vanne, a tucker, and his man, and two local gentlemen evidently ready to hold to Morgan's dangerous courses, Rice ap Rice of Kilpeck, Sir Charles Morgan's brother-in-law, whose 'finger' was already 'in as deepe as the beste', and Thomas Quarrell of Wormbridge. 'The capteyne of them', however, was one Thomas ap Richard (or Prichard) of New Grange, in the parish of Dore but a mile or less from Treville Park. It cannot be said that the attempts made so far to identify this Prichard genealogically have been satisfactory. The Bishop of Hereford described him as 'a man of Sir Roger Bodenham's', an ambiguous phrase which Professor A. H. Dodd has interpreted[4] as meaning that he was one of the Bodenham household. But such an explanation is intrinsically unlikely: this Prichard was plainly a man of some importance, having lands and stock of his own, and Rotherwas, in any case, was many miles off. He may have been of The Grange in Skenfrith, as suggested by John Hobson Matthews,[5] in which parish there were Bodenham lands.[6] Whoever he was (and this point must necessarily be discussed further in another context), it was he who had mustered the forces, man by man, worked them up to a pitch of enthusiasm, and even prepared for counter-attacks upon himself by dispersing his cattle upon other men's lands. His chief lieutenant, in action and in conclave, was Philip Giles of Winnall, another participant in the earlier scenes. It was alleged afterwards that a hundred men from Monmouthshire were expected to come to William Morgan's aid, and although they did not arrive, the suggestion alone may reinforce the likelihood that Prichard, like Giles, was a Monmouthshire man.

For some reason the trap so carefully prepared was never sprung. Exactly why must be matter for conjecture. The non-arrival of reinforcements from over the county border could not have been material. There were men enough in the valletts to master the Bishop, the magistrates and their posse, particularly under cover of darkness. Perhaps William Morgan, at the last moment, thought well of his chances of escaping punishment, trusting to influential friends and connections and growing suddenly cold at the prospect of further violence. Perhaps, too, the arrival in the Bishop's company of a Sir Roger Bodenham prepared to stretch to a convenient elasticity his family motto of *Veritas liberabit* unsettled him as he fidgeted uneasily in the house. Sir Roger was certainly a party to many of the secrets of recusancy, and so well-tried a double-dealer may have counselled against making the breach irrevocable. All that is known is that a message reached Thomas Prichard in The Cockett to the effect that the magistrates had arrived (which he well knew) and that the men in ambush were required to disperse. It may have been Prichard's compliance at this point that gave the Bishop cause to suspect that Sir Roger's relationship with him was that of master and man.

Nevertheless, on whatever advice the ambush was called off, Morgan's side of the affair was mismanaged. No preparations seem to have been made, for instance, against a search of the house. The magistrates were allowed to come upon a number of incriminating letters, some at least written by Morgan himself and as yet undispatched, one a note written by Dr. Harley warning Morgan of his impending arrest, and one a manifesto to the justices drawn up by Cadwallader the priest. Although only William

Morgan himself and a sojourner in the house, Francis Foster, alias Bishop, of Warwickshire,[7] who was known to have attended mass at Whitfield, were there and then taken into custody, the magistrates on their return to Hereford routed out Dr. Harley and, on the evidence of the warning note, made him prisoner too.

In the darkness of Treville Park was better fortune. Thomas Prichard, Philip Giles, Thomas Quarrell and Rice ap Rice, balked at the last minute in their preparations, went into hiding. Few of their party were caught, only the small fry, who turned informer. On June 13 the Bishop was complaining that neither Rice ap Rice nor Roger Cadwallader, the latter wanted mainly because of the manifesto that had been discovered, was anywhere to be found. Rice, however, had not long to run before the ominous word *apprehended* appeared against his name. The Marsh brothers, Leonard and William, soon found their way into the net, together with John Phillips of Kivernoll, wanted for his part in the affray on the Hereford road. But of Thomas Prichard, Philip Giles,[8] Thomas Quarrell, Thomas Price and others among the more determined of the fugitives, there was neither word nor sight.

Meanwhile in Hereford the Bishop was making what play he could with the captured documents and interrogating each of his prisoners in turn. Harley denied authorship of the warning note until comparison with another manuscript which was undeniably in his hand forced him to concede the point. Morgan, however, was obstinately uninformative: he had no idea who sent the letter: he was given it by a young girl, and that was all he knew. Unfortunately for his fellow-prisoners, Foster was of less durable stuff. He acknowledged that Morgan had shown him the letter and told him it came from Harley.

Beyond this, however, the examiners were not very successful. William Morgan made a statement, optimistically called a confession, of which the Bishop bitterly reported that 'in my opinion there is not one word true'. He and Harley were accordingly sent up to London, while Foster and such small fry as had then been taken were retained for further examination on the spot.

The campaign of the Bishop and the other justices, though by good luck well begun, did not prosper. The heavily-wooded nature of the terrain and the nearness of Monmouthshire, 'almost wholly corrupted' according to the Bishop, seriously hindered operations against the southern end of the recusant axis at The Darren. On June 13 Dr. Bennett reported that on the Sunday previous, that is, the one immediately following the fiasco in Treville Park, three hundred persons had assembled for mass at the little chapel on the Monnow bank with arms in their hands. Inviting trouble, the majority of them had lingered on there over the Monday and Tuesday awaiting its arrival. Among these were William Hugh of Monmouthshire, with bow and arrows, and servants of the household of William Vaughan of Llanrothal, who had died in 1588 but whose mother, widow and sister were all fervent recusants.[9] There were James, his shepherd, with a forest bill and a long hanger, Rice, his bailiff, similarly armed, and John and Evan Jenkin, his men, with anything they could lay their hands on. But the occasion did not offer. Official dilatoriness was more than a match for battle temper of this sort. One of the Bishop's apparitors who ventured too close was roughly handled, but nobody else put in an appearance. James, Rice, John and Evan, like the rest, had to go back to their usual labours, where their faithfulness was in as great demand. The rebels, however, kept in touch with each other, and their subsequent actions suggest a degree of organization. Whoever laid the information of the mass-in-arms was politic enough not to notice rebels of gentlemanly rank. Either that or all such kept under cover. Who the leader of these rustics was, therefore, cannot be determined. If Thomas Prichard was really of Skenfrith, his name would stand in rank as well as any. At least he had the capacity both to challenge authority and to use the terrain. But a more productive guess might lead uphill to Oldfield in Garway, whose master, William Mynors, had married Florence, only daughter and sole heiress of the late William Vaughan of Llanrothal. He was afterwards alleged to be deeply involved.

The sequence of events thereafter is uncertain. Probably there were several brushes between the recusants and parties sent out by the justices, without success to the latter. The rebels continued to protest their absolute loyalty to the King and his service, provided they were not harassed on the score of their religion. The purely physical problem of dealing with them, questions of royal policy apart, was proving too hard a nut for the episcopal teeth. Dr. Bennett put his dilemma succinctly enough. 'If we go out with few', he said, 'we shall be beaten home; if we levy any strength, we are descried, and they are all fled into woods, and there they will lurk until the assises be past.'

On the evening of Wednesday, June 19, however, the justices made their biggest effort yet. Sir James Scudamore, William Rudhall, Rowland Vaughan and Thomas Kyrle of Walford,[10] strongly accompanied, searched The Darren and villages adjoining, house by house, all that night and the day following, making a thirty-mile sweep along the borders of Monmouthshire. They found 'altars, images, books of superstition, relics of idolatry', but hardly a living soul, apart from an occasional child or old woman. The villages were desolate. The entire population had fled westwards and southwards, into an even more unpredictable Wales.

Only one man fell into the hands of the posse and, according to the Bishop's story, nothing to the purpose could be gleaned from him. A strong oral tradition has persisted, however, with the telling support of the Franciscan friary at Perthir, a mile or so down the Monnow from Llanrothal, that the man seized was an outlawed priest named Ainsworth (or some name like it)[11] whom the justices' party surprised in his hide-out in the Darren woods and beheaded on the spot. According to the tale, the rock thereabouts was stained with his blood, as indeed were many of the stones in the stream below; the place could be detected quite clearly as late as 1840. Thomas Abbot, a secular priest of Monmouth, writing to Bishop Hedley in 1889, stated that he had by him one of the small stones 'strongly marked, and it becomes especially bright after soaking the stone in water for a few minutes'. His fellow-Catholic, John Hobson Matthews, more cautious, contented himself with remarking, in his continuation of Duncumb's *County History*, that the stones were 'spotted with a crimson something – some say it is a minute fungus – which is not found in the larger brook'. At the spot called 'The Priest's Well' there are to this day some stones so affected.

This, of course, is not history. But oral traditions are not often entirely without foundation. If it be conceded that such a summary execution could have taken place, there is still a confusion about the date to be resolved. Despite the assurance of Father Cronin, who printed Thomas Abbot's letter, that the accounts of Abbot and John Hobson Matthews are 'similar', it is immediately obvious to the casual reader that whereas the former ascribed the incident to 1605, the latter related it to the violent scare of the Titus Oates allegations of 1679. As if intentionally to confuse the local wiseacres, a Scudamore was the probable instrument of violence on both occasions. There are a number of reasons, however, why the story should be refused relevance to the year 1605. The first is purely negative: Abbot's details show no more than that he had read the State Papers. There is nothing to connect the going out of Scudamore, Rudhall, Vaughan and Kyrle with so summary an act. Secondly, the climate of opinion in 1605 and the difficult position of the justices would have militated strongly against violence of this kind, from which there would certainly have been repercussions. None is reported. The same objection is plainly not valid in 1679. The rabidly anti-Catholic Captain Scudamore who uncovered the Jesuit College at The Cwm in that year was much more in character as an executioner than were Spenser's *Sir Scudamour*, the impecunious and trimming Vaughan, and Rudhall and Kyrle, senior and respected gentleman of the shire. Thirdly, both the absence of the name Ainsworth (or anything like it) from the very complete list of priests at large in the neighbourhood in 1604 and 1605, and the fact that the Franciscan cause at Perthir, where the tradition was chiefly kept alive and commemorated annually by a pilgrimage to The Priest's Well, itself dated from 1680, weigh the scales heavily in favour of the later date. Conclusive, perhaps, is the fact that in 1679 there *was* connected with The Cwm a priest named Harcourt, alias Aylworth, who had a remarkable escape from capture by hiding for seven hours under a table in an entrance hall full of soldiery, and who subsequently, in September 1679, died in Holland of stress and privation. Here, however, confusion becomes really master: Father William Harcourt, alias Waring, alias Barrow, also connected with the College of St. Francis Xavier, was one of the five priests hanged, drawn and quartered at Tyburn in June 1679 at the height of the execration raised by Titus Oates, and his end, bloody and summary as it was, must somehow have become entangled in local tradition with that of Harcourt, alias Aylworth (less exactly Ainsworth), who later, perhaps after a decade or two, had his associative Tyburn transferred, willy-nilly, to the banks of Monnow itself. Oral tradition, therefore, is in this instance a bemused and tortuous guide, and the legend of the Darren Brook must forthwith be given its discharge from this narrative.

Reality saw the justices' party returning crestfallen from their intensive search. In London evil rumour was at work. An unofficial report reached the Court on Sunday, June 23, that the Bishops of Hereford and Llandaff had not only been resisted but pursued for their lives. A thousand Catholics were reported in arms at one spot alone, and a full-scale rebellion was feared. A less neurotic appraisal of the situation, dispatched by Dr. Bennett on Saturday, June 22, doubtless reached London early the following week, but by this time there were in all probability some minds in the Council for which any dispatch from the Bishop was no more than a bungle excused. It was at this juncture, on June 29, that the Venetian ambassador included in his dispatch the news that the 'Council meets every day and contrary to his practice the King is present'.

Undoubtedly the season of buck-passing was over. It was now absolutely necessary for the Council to produce gestures more positive than a collective shrug and an expression compounded, in almost equal parts, of hope and burdensome anxiety.

NOTES

[1] This word is not recorded in any of the main dialect dictionaries but appears to mean a dip in the ground, or dell. Other instances in Herefordshire, as Lye Vallets near Lye Court, Knapton Green, some eight miles NNW of Hereford, Lingen Vallet Wood, near Lingen Castle, North Herefordshire, and Lyngham Vallet, near Croft Castle, indicate that it was frequently found in proximity to a great house or castle, and usually in association with a wood or thicket. These facts suggest a derivation from *vallum*.

[2] A local variant of 'the Cockpit'.

[3] 'Dower Stoone', several times referred to in *S.P.* 14, Vol. XIV, 52, ii, seems to have meant the present Abbey Dore, and not the modern parish of Dorstone, some dozen miles away.

[4] Trans. Cymmrodorion, 1937: *Wales and The Scottish Succession* p. 221.

[5] Pub. Catholic Record Society, Miscellanea, II (1906) p. 290. Bradney, op. cit., Vol. I. p. 72, however, makes no mention of a house called The Grange in Skenfrith or of any Thomas Pritchard there. A commission regarding heriots held on Sept. 15, 1606, in the parishes of Grosmont and Llangua (ibid.) revealed one tenement heriotable, and one not, belonging to a Thomas Prichard. This suggests Prichard of The Grange in Campston, quoted by *Llyfr Baglan*, p. 72. There was a Thomas Prichard of this family (ibid., p. 192) who married Anne, daughter of William Morgan of Gwerngochyn and was related on his mother's side to the Mynors of Treiago.

[6] At Blackbrook, held by Thomas Bodenham, younger brother of Sir Roger (Bradney, op. cit., Vol. II, Pt. I., p. 128). Prichard may have been a tenant.

[7] Little evidence of the identity of this man is forthcoming. The ninth daughter of Simon Mylborne of Tillington, Herefordshire, was married to a John Bishop of Worcestershire (*Llyfr Baglan*, p. 45). It is possible, even if not likely, that this Foster was Francis Foster, subsequently O.S.B., who was trained at the English College, Douai, and later at Rome, proceeding to the English mission in 1598. If so, he was the son of Thomas Foster of Tonge, Co. Salop, and brother-in-law of Edward, Lord Stafford. Gillow, Vol. II, pp. 324–5.

[8] Giles, however, was in custody by July and gave evidence against Rice Griffiths. *Cal. of Salis. MSS.*, XVII, pp. 455–6.

[9] Vaughan's mother was formerly Maud Cox of Norton in Skenfrith: his (second) wife Elizabeth, daughter of Sir Thomas Herbert of Wonastow and widow of Watkin Powell. (G. T. Clark, op. cit., p. 266): and his sister Elizabeth wife of Walter Vaughan of Cophill. Pub. Catholic Record Society, Miscellanea, II, p. 293.

¹⁰ In the Bishop's letter, printed in Dodd's *Church History*, Vol. IV., Appendix p. 100, the name appears as Reole, which it certainly resembles in *S.P.* 14, Vol. XIV, 52. But John Hobson Matthews, in Pub. Catholic Record Society, Miscellanea, II, p. 289, is undoubtedly right in reading it as Kyrle.

¹¹ The name rests mainly on the authority of Bishop Hendren, at one time an alumnus of Perthir, who in 1808, when he first went there, *thought* that the old people of the locality said it was Ainsworth, or something like it. Cronin, op. cit.

CHAPTER V

Pacification and Dissimulation

THE Council, during those late June days, although disquieted and under the royal eye, were not concerned to admit their own previous procrastination. It was much easier to blame the magistrates. They had 'failed to carry out their orders with that dexterity which was contemplated by the King and Council'. Instead, 'with rigorous fury', they had arrested hundreds of persons. A long debate ensued. Some, and among them the King, always easily alarmed, were for arms. One or two, doubtless, would have endorsed the comment of Sir Henry Neville that 'if we mean not to grant all, we were as good deny all, and put them to an Issue betimes'. But others, and these the majority, were afraid that force would fail in so sturdily recusant a county, with the result that the King's authority would be further undermined and the revolt be spread more widely still. It was better 'to proceed cautiously, and to lay the blame for what had occurred upon the magistrates, who either could not or would not execute their orders in the proper spirit'. Some of those who pressed this point may conceivably, if a recent apologist for the Gunpowder Plotters be given any credit, have had a more subtle reason for treating the culprits gently. It might well be a pity to take the fire too soon out of a better Plot.[1] But in the nature of things it is hardly likely that such an allegation could come to proof.

After long deliberation the Council decided upon their masterstroke. They would send down the Earl of Worcester, by reputation a stiff Papist in Elizabeth's reign[2] but Master of the Horse under James and exempt from all penalties by the King's personal favour, to talk to the recusant leaders and quell the revolt. The Earl, whose seat was at Raglan, was in any case the natural over-lord of the affected district, which was on the borders of the Lord-Lieutenancy that he had excepted for himself in 1602 out of the jurisdiction of the Council in the Marches. Because of this, and because of his Catholicism, however tepid in the present, the recusant leaders would, it was hoped, defer to his authority. Of what had happened to Sir Herbert Croft, if he ever travelled down to Herefordshire, there is no mention.

Edward Somerset, fourth Earl of Worcester, was almost cer-tainly a more complex personality than he appeared to many contemporaries. Considered the best horseman and tilter of the day, he was ready in the provision of jests for the King's lighter moments. The bonhomie with which the whole Court was familiar was both the means to royal favour and the cover for the more purposeful side of his nature. It may be noted, for instance, that Thomas Williams of Trefriw, in the preface to his *Welsh Grammar* published in 1632, described him as one 'who does not hesitate to speak Welsh and to cherish and magnify it in a dearly British manner', coupling him for this with Sir Edward Stradling, 'the chief cherisher of our Welsh language in South Wales'. There were long periods during the early months of 1605 when Sir Philip Herbert, the junior Secretary of State, who, in the words of James himself, 'hath conjured all the devils here with his Welsh tongue', and the Earl of Worcester were the King's only compan-ions on his East Midland progress. The much less Cymric 'little beagle' remained in London. Philip Herbert, younger brother of the third Earl of Pembroke and a notably handsome man, was from the early days of the reign one of King James's secondary favourites: during the spring of 1605 *his* progress was one of acquisition as well as sport: to the lordship of Denbigh, granted to him in 1604, he added the earldom and the castle of Montgomery (the latter to the deep annoyance of Edward, future Lord Herbert of Cherbury, whose family had lived in it for a hundred years).

Ostensibly James took Edward Somerset and Philip Herbert with him to the East Midlands because of their interest and prowess in field sports. But it was a time wormed through with anxiety and jealousy for Salisbury, who as much lacked virility as he cherished reason and composure. More than one of James's own notes to his senior Secretary betrays a desire to irritate. Herbert, he wrote some time in March, 'is secretary of our corporation that is of fools, horses and dogs'. Close observers at Court were perhaps not far wrong in conceiving the folly to be no less than the animal complement: the pan-British sentiments afoot in certain Catholic circles on such a progress had opportunity to raise a gallop.

Worcester's part, both with the King and without, offers considerable difficulty. Neither his real motives, nor the attitude of the Council to his known record as a Catholic in the previous reign, are sufficiently displayed. To say that he treated his faith as a private matter, as does Professor A. H. Dodd,[3] explains little: he was here placed in a situation where its relevance to his public actions was vital. Even if he had all the outward marks of the *politique*, it is still important to know precisely how he was regarded by the King, the Council and the Catholic interest. It may be that James thought to use him, as the Earl of Northampton had been used, as a springe to catch woodcocks, or as a Catholic pipe close to the royal ear tuned in particular to the key of distant threats and murmurs. The Court may have regarded him merely as one the continuance of whose royal and public favour must necessarily depend absolutely upon the acceptance and execution of the command of the King-in-Council. Worcester, on the contrary, may have felt himself a loftier Rice Griffiths, a pipe whose main vent was in his lord-lieutenancies of Glamorgan and Monmouth, serving his more extreme co-religionaries in the former Essex manner. The evidence, if not conclusive, at least puts him under suspicion of this.

Howbeit, his arrival at Raglan on or about Saturday, June 29[4] heralded the last stage of the disturbance. It had lasted already for over six weeks, with small credit earned either by the Council or the magistrates, apart from the arrest of William Morgan and a few more. Over the failure locally, however, the Bishop of Hereford was now disposed to be truculent. Tired of being everybody's whipping-boy, he had declared on June 22 that the refusal to grant him a commission ecclesiastical, applied for as long ago as the March previous, was the root cause of the débâcle in his diocese. Without such a commission the magistrates were at the King's mercy for any blood shed in the discharge of their duty, and this 'maketh some go out in cold blood'.[5] Referring bitterly and pointedly to those 'unwilling that any authority of that nature should pass further than their own hands', he concluded his letter to the Earl of Salisbury as follows: 'If I may have it (the commission ecclesiastical) I will do the service: if I may not, *liberavi animam meam*. I will live the more private, and let the blame light where it will'.

Bancroft had his *tu quoque*. And it is evident, from the Bishop's tone, that he was conscious of enmities to which his own truculence might appeal. With whatever backing the Earl of Worcester should arrive in Herefordshire, it was unlikely that the Bishop would accord him a walk-over. It was the rebels, as at least some of the Council had intended, who were the more puzzled and taken aback by the new arrival.

But first the censure. On the Monday morning after the Earl's arrival the Bishop and justices attended him at Raglan to have their knuckles rapped. They were first treated (by a reputed Catholic) to a discourse on the care of King James for 'God's true religion and suppressing of Popish superstition' and to a complaint of the widespread misrepresentation from which the royal policy suffered in the diocese of Hereford. For this, of course, there were two causes: one, want of good teaching and preaching (the Bishop's fault): the other, negligence on the part of the justices. After this neat acquittal of the royal method of prevarication came the expected humble or inaudible replies. 'This care of His Majesty to preserve the peace of the country increased their affections, if it were possible.' Lord Zouche, President of the

Council in the Marches, on whom the royal mandate to the Earl of Worcester to extend temporarily the jurisdiction of his lieu-tenancies into Herefordshire undoubtedly cast some reflection, wrote from Bath excusing himself (as was now customary with him) on the grounds of ill-health but proffering any service of which he was capable.[6] The formal acceptance of blame was over.

Thereupon orders were given for a general and concurrent search on the evening of the following day (Tuesday), every justice to be responsible for his own immediate area. It does not appear that anything or anybody of importance was caught in this wide-spread net, nor perhaps did Worcester expect much catch of it.[7] He himself was fisherman-in-chief, with the use of a different bait. Everything depended on the attitude taken by the recusants to his personal mission.

The second stage of his public activity was timed to begin on Monday, July 8, when a progress in state was made into Hereford-shire, followed by a series of simultaneous searches along both sides of the troublesome Monmouthshire border. The first six days after his arrival, however, had been spent by the Earl in mak-ing contact with the recusants by means of 'persons underhand'. In this procedure there is little doubt that he was instructed and abetted by Sir Roger Bodenham, ostensibly in his capacity as Deputy-Lieutenant for the Shire. He had always known a great deal more of the affair than he had disclosed to the Bishop of Hereford or his fellow-justices. Contact was made almost imme-diately, and first with Rice Griffiths, whom Sir Roger brought to the Earl. That Worcester should, in a dispatch to the Earl of Salisbury, both refer openly to the Archbishop of Canterbury's protection of Griffiths and admit that he had been told about him by the Archbishop before he left London may suggest that the Archbishop's attitude and policy were endorsed by many of the Council. But the inclusion in his letter of a remark of Sir Roger Bodenham's that those who in public admitted they were priests 'did great harm in the country' and the seemingly ingenuous ex-pression of surprise that Griffiths had no real information to offer

are undoubtedly smooth criticisms of that policy, probably for
Salisbury's private ear. It is difficult not to feel that Worcester,
with Bodenham's advice, was playing a very cunning hand. He
wished quietly to discredit the Bancroft–Griffiths axis, whether or
not it were the Archbishop who was being fooled. No long-term
benefit for Catholics was that way likely to emerge. Better to lie
close, use trustier vents – himself perhaps – and wait. Meanwhile
he could afford to joke about having been at confession with
Griffiths, with the usual relationship this time in reverse. Such a
taunt left Griffiths's pretensions sadly draggled: the Earl, on the
other hand, was, for a one-time Catholic, the most open and jolly
of fellows, one from whom the priesthood could no longer count
on anything much by way of reverence.

Meanwhile, Salisbury was assured, all priests had fled the district. Rice Griffiths himself, having been privately rated (or so
Worcester would have it believed), was allowed to set off south-
westwards for Glamorgan, from which shire he promised all
possible intelligence.

After this contact a movement towards a general surrender set
in. Most of the recusants sought Worcester's mercy, 'having
waded too farre already'. One or two were committed to prison.
The less seriously involved were remonstrated with on theological
grounds and 'from stiffe Recusants they are converted and become
new Scholars in Christes Schoole'. Thus the allegedly local cor-
respondent in *The Late Commotion*, whose notions of the methods
one Catholic would use in quietening and pacifying others are
quaint.

The Earl of Worcester had undoubtedly decided, either before
he left London, or after consultation with Sir Roger Bodenham,
that the affair could be played down. The line to take was this:
priests and others who might suffer serious punishment had got
away and were out of reach: those who could be reached were un-
important tools in the hands of the real instigators. In the words of
the Venetian ambassador, who stood near enough to catch the
impressions Worcester's dispatches created at Court, the distur-

bance was 'far inferior in importance to what had been represented'. The Earl had 'put a few fellows of the baser sort into prison, more to show that he had done something than because they deserved punishment'. The fuss, indeed, was about very little. Worcester's personal report took care to point out that he was 'as weary with examinations of silly creatures' as ever in his life.

If there is a point in all this that arouses curiosity, it is the insistence upon the guilt of James Morris, alias Jones, who, together with other priests, had not waited to see whether the Earl was bringing them a dispensation for past follies or the Bishop and magistrates a certification of diplomatic services rendered. Opinion was that he had gone to London. But this may have been mentioned in the Earl's dispatch mainly because Morris, alias Jones, was already incriminated by the letters taken in Morgan's house, and confirmation of his having gone to London was expected. Much depends on what, if anything, Morgan had admitted in Hereford before his departure for the Tower, and whether or not the Earl had seen the depositions.

It must be confessed that Worcester's report raises grave suspicions. This hushing-up may have been desired by the King: it was certainly intended by the Archbishop of Canterbury, the credit of whose policy of infiltration was threatened, and astutely achieved, if perhaps for reasons at odds with those of either King or Archbishop, by one whose religious credentials and personal activities have been insufficiently examined.

NOTES

[1] *Vide* the thesis put forward in Hugh Ross Williamson, *The Gunpowder Plot*, *passim*, that the Plot was known to the Earl of Salisbury, if not positively encouraged by him, from its inception. If that were so, it would not serve to have the horrific revelation of the Powder Plot and its probable effect on public opinion forestalled and set off at half-cock by a distant and less luridly explosive affair in the Welsh Marches.

[2] Precisely why Williamson, ibid., p. 171, refers to Worcester as 'the bitter anti-Catholic who . . . organized the search for Jesuits in Worcestershire' is far

from clear. He appears to have taken Worcester's stagey dispatches at their face value. His anxiety, in any case, to castigate all opponents of the Jesuits colours too much of his argument.

³ Op. cit., Trans. Cymmrodorion, 1948. In his article in *The Dictionary of Welsh Biography*, he describes Worcester simply as 'a politique', a view evidently shared by Bishop Mathew.

⁴ The divergences between authorities on this point are considerable: Sir Henry Neville (*Memoirs, Winwood*, Vol. II, p. 77) wrote on June 21 that the Earl had already been sent (unless it mean that the decision to send him had already been taken): P. Sanford (Lodge, op. cit., III, 293) on June 23 reported that he was immediately to go: the Venetian Ambassador (*Cal. of S.P.* Ven. X, p. 390) wrote on June 29 that he had just heard that the Earl was to be sent: Mr. E. R. of Hereford (*The Late Commotion*, p.32) that he arrived at Raglan a few days after June 29. The Earl himself referred on July 5 (*Cal. of Salis., MSS.*, Pt. XVII, p. 304) to 'the shortness of my being in these parts'.

⁵ S.P. 14, Vol. XIV, 52. This hardly sounds like the complaint of one whose fellow-magistrates had just butchered a priest. It makes the applicability of *The Legend of the Darren Brook* to the year 1605 even less likely.

⁶ In the course of the six months preceding he had written half a dozen times to the Earl of Salisbury asking for his release from the Presidency. On June 20 he wrote again commenting on the fact that Worcester rather than he had been given the commission in Herefordshire and adding that he 'had advertisement that a further matter was in working that my said Lord should receive my place – whereof I was exceeding glad'.

⁷ On Friday, July 5 he reported merely that 'the return is not altogether come to my hands'.

CHAPTER VI

A Confession, a Deal of Bewilderment, and Some Bitterness

TUMULT in Herefordshire and Monmouthshire was at an end, and in the sudden and surprising silence there its echoes farther off could be heard still reverberating. In London, it is true, they were muffled by prison walls, and little enough was audible at Court. But the original note, though fallen, was not quite toneless yet, although the prisoners had reached the capital a full fortnight before.

William Morgan, the enigmatic spokesman of the Allensmore road, was still maintaining the rigid aspect of a stone required to produce blood. On June 17 he had been examined by the Council, but had had difficulty in remembering anything clearly. The following day Chief Justice Popham, Mr. Justice Williams and Attorney-General Coke examined him again. Of this trio, Sir David Williams, who in 1600 had purchased the estate of Gwerny-fed in Breconshire, was the one to check any confession against an intimate knowledge of the affairs of the Marches. As recently as the April previous he had been one of the Judges of Assize at Usk. Popham's elaborate system of informers had made him, too, an interrogator in whose hearing a slip in the facts was unwise. Coke's part was that of rhetoric: his browbeatings seem to have convinced Morgan that at least an appearance of co-operation was advisable. Sir William Waad reported on June 18 that 'his memory serves him better this morning than yesterday' and suggested that he be moved from his temporary confinement at the Hermitage, Charing Cross, to the Tower, where alone of the London prisons he could be kept without news or contact with other prisoners. To the Tower and Waad's own keeping he was accordingly transferred. Among his fellows there in ward were Lord Cobham, Sir Walter Raleigh and Thomas Bywater the Puritan.

The evaluation of his confession, however, remains a difficult matter. In comparison with Dr. Harley, also in custody, who acknowledged 'nothing to any purpose', William Morgan was considered talkative. But Harley may have been fortuitously involved. He may have *known* nothing. So much, in any case, depends on what the Council already knew from the captured letters. Even more is judgment dependent on the identity and social status of William Morgan. Nevertheless, the main impression left by the breviat of his admissions on June 18 is that with a great show of reluctance he was giving very little away. Yes, he acknowledged having received a note by a maid, but he did not know from whom it came. He guessed it was from Harley, and he admitted showing it to Foster. He denied having seen the manifesto to the justices before he was shown it by the Bishop of Hereford, but, yes, he did recognize Cadwallader's handwriting, because his father at Stretton Sugwas was a near neighbour of his. That Cadwallader was a priest he knew only by hearsay. Again, he did remember now that James Morris, alias Jones (whose name had eluded him earlier), had been in his house and had counselled him to do something in defence of the Catholic cause 'Because the Bishop ment to take some hard course with him and the Catholiques'. The promptings behind this answer are almost audible.

The most significant feature of Morgan's examination, however, was his denial that any principal and important Catholics were involved. The only names he would give were those of James Coles, one of the Marsh brothers (probably William), Francis Foster (all of these were in custody), William Mynors of Oldfield, Garway, Powell his brother-in-law (one of three possible Powells and not with certainty identifiable)¹ and Thomas Sais of Withington, Kilpeck.² Of these only Mynors, the second son of Treiago, was of any appreciable rank. Coles was a weaver and Marsh either that or a labourer. Sais was a yeoman farmer with gentlemanly pretensions. Foster, as a stranger, is difficult to classify, and suggestions as to his identity must be deferred. The list, in any case, is strangely attenuated. An uneasy choice between two alternatives remains: either that Morgan was a man of no great rank himself, even if a natural leader, and was telling the entire and pitiful truth, or that his admissions were no more than a recognition of evidence already in the Council's possession, and that he had no intention of volunteering even the smallest extension of it.

Morgan's statement that he recognized Cadwallader's handwriting had been made at Hereford, when he was first confronted with the manifesto to the justices. The Bishop then gave it as his opinion that in his confession there was 'not one word true'. Probably he would have had little cause to change his verdict had he been present at the hearing in London. The dragging answers given by the prisoner enlarged only by a hair's breadth the point of incrimination. Two of the intended recipients of the captured letters, he let it be understood, were John Smith, then a prisoner in the Gatehouse but presumably soon to be set at liberty (since he was expected to represent Catholic grievances at Court), and Rice Griffiths (the Magog referred to) who was to use his good offices with the Archbishop to smooth away all offence. The other letters were superscribed with the names of their recipients. The persons mentioned as coming up to London, he said, were James Morris, alias Jones, and himself. So the little circle of names grew scarcely at all.

Meanwhile, in Herefordshire, Dr. Bennett had interrupted the shushings of the Earl of Worcester by suddenly arresting Rice Griffiths. No certain date can be assigned for this piece of irritable counterpoint. The first mention of it was in the Bishop's letter of August 9 to the Earl of Salisbury, and it can hardly have happened earlier than the second week in July. If Griffiths ever left for Glamorgan after his interview with the Earl of Worcester, he evidently did not stay there long and his suspicions of personal danger must have been completely allayed by Worcester's attitude, both public and private. Both he and his lay advisers, however, had underestimated the Bishop, who was not a man to be cowed for more than a moment by the voice from Court. Irritated beyond measure by the wide currency given to the report that his knuckles had been rapped by the Earl, knowing that the Archbishop of Canterbury would pull his own chestnuts out of the fire without a care for burnt fingers in Hereford, and hearing that Griffiths was going round openly advertising Bancroft's interest in minimizing the affair, Dr. Bennett decided that he had nothing to lose by being bold. Griffiths, therefore, was taken, rigorously examined with the help of Paul Delahay, and published abroad as a double-dealer. It is clear from the depositions of the numerous Catholics questioned before this hasty tribunal that the officially-reformed priest had emboldened his fellows by emphasizing his own access to the Archbishop, and in particular by bringing the Bishop of Hereford's plans against them to nothing by his own foreknowledge. That he subsequently earned the distrust of many Catholics, who either felt that the affrays were largely caused by his self-assured misrepresentations or objected to his 'lewdness' (a word that in the early seventeenth century appears to have meant 'irresponsibility' or 'wildness' in a general rather than a sexual sense) and found in him a convenient scapegoat, also seems likely. But the charge that he was an *agent provocateur*, repeated in subsequent Catholic apologia, is certainly not substantiated. On the contrary, there is every indication that whoever it was he had fooled, it was not the Catholics of Webtree and Wormelow.

Perhaps the knowledge that some charges had been made of itself produced others. In any case, Griffiths was held for the Assizes.

But the Archbishop, highly incensed at the fate of his protégé and fearful for the credit of his recent policy, was not finished with yet. When, within a few weeks, the Assizes came round, there came letters from him requesting the judges to 'forbear him'. Griffiths was to be dismissed on bond to appear in the Court of King's Bench at the next term and to report to the Archbishop without delay. This long-distance bout ended, therefore, with another knock for the Bishop and a parade of his freedom by Griffiths, 'who walks abroad triumphantly'.

Though balked, Dr. Bennett was not comfortless. He did not fail to transmit to the Council a breviat of the accusations and evidence against Rice Griffiths and to comment bitterly on a policy which rewarded undoubted offenders 'with a plume of feathers'. The recent affrays, he contended, *had* been serious, whoever reported to the contrary. 'Such carriage of matters is the next way to make men cold in future service.' As for Griffiths, 'he never did service worth the least thanks ... Some may think his offences may be tolerated, so it be to do service; but I hold it a bad policy to permit a man to commit a blasphemous act (as the mass is) to the end to do another service.' So, in the old quarrel of means and ends, the man on the spot, howsoever unsaintly, was able in his turn to do a little lofty knuckle-rapping.

The bastions of official silence make the conclusion of this duel conjectural. No more was heard of Rice Griffiths and he was probably spared his appearance before the King's Bench. The Bishop of Hereford's wounds were salved by letters of appreciation from the Council. Of the mopping-up operations only a few traces remain. John Smith of Kilpeck, the other equivocator, who had been a prisoner in the Gatehouse for reasons which do not appear, had been released in July and was once more in Herefordshire. Whether released on this condition or no, he had agreed with the Bishop and Paul Delahay to assist in laying some of the fugitives by the heels. A little while later a letter from Edwards, the seminary priest, was intercepted. He lay hidden in the house of one Staney, in Monmouthshire. Delahay, with the privity of the Bishop, had the house surrounded and searched. But the secret vaults and passages were too many. Edwards could not be ferreted out, and afterwards got clean away. Nothing was heard of Cadwallader and the other fugitives.

The ill-success of the hunters continued. An ostensible merchant, giving the name of David Butler (a surname which was one of the aliases of Thomas Lister the Jesuit) and accompanied by a boy, had sailed from Cardiff in *The Speedwell*, out of Bridgwater and bound for Portugal. Delayed by a contrary wind, the ship put in at the little port of Mongey in Galicia (probably to be identified with the modern Mugia), where the passengers were persuaded ashore. The captain of *The Speedwell*, with the unwholesome righteousness of a man recently pardoned for piracy,[3] had kept them under observation, and now availed himself of their absence. He had their baggage searched, abstracted a letter he found there and substituted a blank sheet of paper for it, which blank Butler duly dispatched by the boy to Madrid. *The Speedwell* thereupon carried the *soi-disant* merchant back to Minehead, where the portreeve was informed. The fact that the letter abstracted proved to be from James Morris, alias Jones, the seminary priest, to Father Joseph Cresswell the Jesuit moved the portreeve no quicker than usual. Broils in Wales, where there were always broils of one sort or another, did not suggest to him the need for urgent and immediate action. Indeed, knowing that Chief Justice Popham was then at his house in Wellington, not far away, he judged the safest course to be to send him the evidence and await instructions. In the result, Butler, now well aware that he was a marked man, succeeded in slipping out of the port and back to Wales, where the Lord Chief Justice expected, without justification, that Smith would lay him by the heels. The last-named 'for his pains', as Paul Delahay reported, 'is so wellbeloved amongst them, that he is like to remain awhile unabsolved of any of his ghostly fathers'.

Where John Smith failed, however, more normal means finally succeeded. On August 31 Chief Justice Popham was able to report that Sir Rowland Morgan had David Butler fast in Cardiff Gaol. Salisbury suggested that he should be shipped back to Somerset and examined by Popham at his own house, but he did not envisage that he could be kept in custody indefinitely. 'We cannot now be so severe as to punish the carrier of letters, peace being concluded with all nations, except it appear that they be receivers of them from ['known priests' struck out] those that they know to to be offenders, or privy to the contents of such stuff as is contained in them.' It was just this point, of course, that was so difficult to prove. Butler might carry stock worth no more than five or six pounds: he might be no merchant at all but solely a carrier for the Jesuits: it was, nevertheless, all but impossible to make 'carrying' a sufficient offence.

What Popham finally made of the affair is not documented, and whether *carrier* proved in the end to be *priest* is equally hidden. Meanwhile, in Herefordshire, the justices had the situation well in hand. The lay recusants were shepherdless and very much lost. Both Cadwallader and Edwards were believed to have left the district, which 'for a while is quite purged of their society'. The arrest of Rice Griffiths, following hard upon the Earl of Worcester's palliations, had much discomfited all but the few who could resolve the contradiction. Most of them did not know what to expect next. Even if it were optimistic to write, as Delahay did, that 'of above 1,000 recusants in this county, the tenth part of them are now scarce left for the Pope, and most of them women', there was no doubt that rebellion was fully scotched.

The conclusion of the affair is as untidy and uncertain as much of the evidence preceding. William Morgan, in whom King and Council had rapidly lost interest of late, came momentarily again under the scrutiny of the Lieutenant of the Tower when he was informed that one of the only two servants whom Lord Cobham had been permitted to keep by him, a man named Morgan, had had access to his namesake, apparently with the connivance of his keeper. For a while, no doubt, Waad wondered whether there *was*, after all, a common thread binding the Herefordshire commotion to the other and more dangerous conspiracies of recent years. But his experienced judgment was soon satisfied. On August 19 he wrote to Salisbury saying that he had made no move to show that he was aware of the contact of Morgan the servant with William Morgan, gent.: 'neither think I it was for any purpose but in kindness, and yet I have appointed him another keeper.' It was no more than a postscript to a tale that was virtually told. King James was able, with only the smallest interval, to resume the prime interest he took in Waad's reports and to savour the most up-to-date comment on the progress and behaviour of the lion cubs in the Tower.

There is a break in the Tower Bills at this point, and since the Registers of the Acts of the Privy Council for this and subsequent years were lost in a fire at Whitehall in 1618,[4] further inquiry is entirely balked.[5] Robert Abbot, Regius Professor of Theology at Oxford and brother of the then Archbishop of Canterbury, asserted in an anti-Jesuit pamphlet of 1613 that Morgan was released from custody after a relatively short imprisonment,[6] and this development, which has an air of strong probability, would have been quite consistent with the low temperature induced in official circles by the Earl of Worcester and the Archbishop. Catholic apologia included an impressive list of severities imposed by the Bishop of Hereford[7] and it was not difficult to obtain credence for the view that Morgan and his followers had had provocation in plenty.

It is, perhaps, little more than a guess that Sir Charles Morgan found his way out of the Fleet at about the same time. He was certainly back at Arkston in 1610, when he was the defendant in a lawsuit about the tithes of Treville.[8] With his consent, and under his indenture and that of his brother Thomas, the lease of the manor of Treville was in January 1614 transferred by John James of Kilpeck and John Philipps of Kivernoll to Sir Walter Pye of The Mynde. In August 1617 Sir Charles, his widowed mother and brothers, made an outright grant of the manor, park and castle of Kilpeck, together with part of the manor of Treville, to Sir Walter Pye and William Scudamore of Ballingham for a consideration of £2,700. Obviously the Morgans were in serious financial straits, and within a year or two Arkston itself was sold to Serjeant Hoskyns of the 'prodigious memorie', who about 1621 exchanged it with Stephen Parry for Moorhampton, not far away. Through Hoskyns, who had been close enough to Dr. Bennett to have him stand as godfather to his son Benedict, the Bishop obtained, over one of the equivocators at least, a sort of posthumous economic revenge. When exactly Sir Charles died does not appear, but since he had no heirs, such of his rights as were left passed to his brother Thomas. His days seem to have run palely towards the end.

The scapegoats, then, came away with no worse than a bloodletting, and returned to their wilderness. Beyond this it would be unwise to go.

NOTES

[1] The documents are confounded with Powells, as with Griffithses. Among those who had attended mass at Whitfield was a John Powell. He had also been one of the party in ambush for the justices near William Morgan's house (*vide* S.P. 14, Vol. XIV, 53, ii) and was now in custody. Richard Powell of Kilpeck, gentleman, named as one of the most dangerous recusants in the diocese, was also a member of the party in ambush (ibid.). William Powell, who attended mass at The Darren and held lands in Garway, married as his second wife Elizabeth, daughter of William Morgan of Kilpeck (*Llyfr Baglan*, p. 243). There is no indication of any relationship to Mynors of Oldfield, but if this should be the *right* Powell and William Morgan of Kilpeck the *right* William Morgan, then the reason for the conspiracy of these particular Catholics becomes plainer.

[2] Thomas ap William ap Rosser ap John ap Howel Sais ap Iorwerth ap Gronow ap David ap Sitsyllt ap Sir Gilbert Winston. *Llyfr Baglan*, pp. 296–7. Withington in 1910 was an old farmhouse in the parish of Kilpeck, showing signs of considerable size and importance, but then converted into workmen's dwellings.

[3] George Escot, captain of *The Speedwell*, was probably identical with George Estcourt, alias Willis, who on February 27, 1605 received a grant of pardon for piracy against certain Venetians. *Cal. of S.P. Domestic*, Vol. XII.

[4] The gap in the Privy Council Registers extends from January 1, 1602 to April 30, 1613. The missing volumes were burned in a fire on January 12, 1618, in which the Banqueting House at Whitehall (under which the Records were kept) was burned to the ground.

[5] It is odd too that the Court Books (Depositions) of the Episcopal Court at Hereford are missing for the years 1602–8, the only break in the series between 1596 and 1673.

F

⁶ 'non multo post libertati restitutus est'. *Antilogia Adversus Apologiam Andreae Eudaemon Ioannis Iesuitae*, p.131.

⁷ Four hundred and nine families in the county alone had been reduced to beggary by the severities of the Bishop of Hereford. Quoted in Lingard, *History of England*, 5th ed., Vol. VII, p. 51.

⁸ John Gwillim, clerk, brought the action, denying both Sir Charles's right to the tithes of Treville and his presumed claim that the font stones in Kilpeck Church belonged originally to the former chapel in Treville Park. Heref. & Mon., 8 Jas. I, 1610. C27 Hil. Term. Also P.R.O. Interrogatories, Jas. I, 1610. The Examination was taken at the Market House of Grosmont on August 29, 1610. Sir Charles presumably won the part of the action concerning tithes.

CHAPTER VII

Who was William Morgan?

BEFORE interpretation, identification. To seek for an explanation of Catholic behaviour in Herefordshire in the summer of 1605, to offer reasons why rebellion, though limited in scope, was also planned and maintained for at least six weeks, will be difficult enough. Without a preliminary attempt to identify its leader it will be impossible. The first question, therefore, is not the less inevitable because it goes on to pose others. It must out. Who *was* 'Master William Morgan of Treble Park'? No single wind would so unfog the scene as one that carried the certain sound of his name and standing. But that wind does not blow. All that we have is the gusty round of possibilities, significant and insignificant, for a moment likely and then not worth the hearing. It is difficult weather when even experience is glad of a guess.

There are two scraps of evidence in the document optimistically called William Morgan's *confession*. At one point he let fall 'That my Lord of Canterbury would take the rescue greeviously because he was his kinsman, and therefore that he woulde deale with one Griffith that was with my Lord to satisfie him, Last the connstable would agravate the matter'. *His kinsman.* Unfortunately this scent disperses at the first step. Richard Bancroft, the Archbishop, was a Lancashireman, born in 1544 of a Farnworth family, and if he had any relatives in the southern marches of Wales, they have not so far been discovered. The ambiguity of the phrase *his kinsman* may perhaps more easily resolve itself into a relationship between the Archbishop and George Wenlond, the Constable. If so, it is no help towards William Morgan.

73

In the same *confession* he averred that 'for anie principall
Catholiques, he knew none, but had speech with William Mynors,
Powell his brother-in-Lawe, and one Sayes'. It would be possible,
if not entirely likely, to interpret this Powell as the brother-in-law
of the speaker (that is, William Morgan) rather than as a relative of
William Mynors. In *Llyfr Baglan* there is mention of a William
Powell, probably of Garway, alive in 1607, who married as his
second wife Elizabeth, the daughter of William Morgan of Kilpeck. Morgan of Treville Park could well have been Morgan of
Kilpeck, but the Powell–Morgan relationship is incorrect and nowhere else in the pedigrees collected and edited by either G. T.
Clark or J. A. Bradney is any Morgan so described. That a
William Morgan of Kilpeck did exist, however, is confirmed by
an entry for December 1604 in one of the manuscripts of the
Hereford Corporation. There James Berrowe, gent., defendant in
an action brought by William Goulston, doctor or plague atten-
dant, asserted that Goulston left his house at the end of a fortnight
for that of William Morgan of Kilpeck, gent. Two of the Kentchurch Court Deeds for 1606 similarly refer to a William Morgan
of Kilpeck, gent. If it could be established that the William Morgans of Treville Park and Kilpeck were one and the same, no great
progress, however, would have been made. Neither of them can
be placed, in family terms, in any of the printed pedigrees. The
second clue, therefore, (if indeed it were one), proves to be useless.

At least one previous attempt, however, has been made to use
the pedigrees to *place* William Morgan. John Hobson Matthews
asserted, not entirely ingenuously, in his continuation of Duncumb's *History of the County of Hereford*, that he was a cousin of
Sir Charles Morgan of Arkston. By this he meant, as he more
cautiously suggested in another place,[1] William Morgan of Blackmoor, a farmhouse a mile or so north-west of Whitfield. The
Morgans of Blackmoor were a cadet branch of the family at
Arkston, being descended from Thomas Morgan, brother to
Charles, Sir Charles's grandfather. This Thomas was still sufficiently alive and full of pretensions in 1602 to obtain a grant from

Camden of a separate coat of arms. That the lion rampant sable, crowned or, on a field argent, which the house of Blackmoor received, marked a genuine rise in status may be doubted, since knowledge of Thomas's descendants is far from complete. According to Bradney, however, he had a second son named William, who would therefore have been cousin to Thomas Morgan of Arkston, Sir Charles's father. *Llyfr Baglan,* compiled in 1607 by John Williams, supposedly an Ergyng man, gave this William as the *third* son of Thomas Morgan of Blackmoor and the Garnons, Garnest, or Gamul heiress[2] to whom the house and lands had descended.

G. T. Clark's *Limbus Patrum* provides an alternative. There William Morgan, in what is clearly a reading of the same pedigree, appears as the third son of Thomas Morgan of Arkston, Sir Charles's younger brother and successor. To accept this would be to make of William Morgan a very young sprig indeed, and a sprig who should have been living at Arkston with his father and uncles. That he should live at the Park Farm (or Whitfield) and be so named without reference to Arkston makes this solution unlikely.

Of the two versions Clark's is, of course, the one to give William Morgan status. With a father at Arkston and the manor dominated by the steady and avuncular shadow of Sir Charles himself, William, with a nominal holding in Treville Park, could well have counted for more than his lands. But Sir Charles's shadow was anything but steady and Clark is clearly wrong. The alternative, of a second or third son of Blackmoor who would have been a cousin to Sir Charles's father (or just possibly to Sir Charles himself)[3] is slightly more plausible. It is not impossible that an adventurer of strong character could, with many of the marks of rank, have taken precedence over Rice ap Rice (Sir Charles's brother-in-law), the Quarrells of Wormbridge, Philipps of Kivernoll, John Griffiths of Kingstone, Sais of Kilpeck and their like, and even over William Mynors of Oldfield, a cadet of the considerable Treiago family. But the Bishop of Hereford's allegations, if they bear but the semblance of truth, make this chance an even longer one. It was not merely that this Morgan had been 'a champion to encourage many'. On the death of Queen Elizabeth, ran the charge, he was one of several who had made the early motions of conspiracy. With John Smith of Kilpeck and Eaton, alias North, the priest, he had talked about taking up arms and the matter had been broached to Sir Charles Morgan. Cadwallader and he had also been privy in some way to Watson's Plot. Such actions are those of a hothead, not of a dependant, and if they suggest only a desire to lead, they seem also to presuppose a sufficiency of rank to make leadership possible. William Morgan was referred to always as of Treville, never of Blackmoor, and the uncertainty even of *Llyfr Baglan* about the descendants of Thomas Morgan hardly suggests that any of the Blackmoor family were well known.

It must be faced. William Morgan of Blackmoor has two major claims to consideration, and only two. The first is particular to him alone. He was on the spot, or remarkably near it. The second applies also to all but one of the William Morgans who follow. The appellation *gent.* (which was usually used of William Morgan of Treville) seems, at least in deeds and official lists, to have been used to show membership of the lesser gentry. Gentlemen of well-known family and status, even when not knights, were usually *Mr.* or *Esquire*. On the other hand, *gent.* was undoubtedly sometimes used of sons not yet in possession of their patrimony: equally certainly it was applied to some members of the magistracy, despite their theoretical right to be called *Esquire*. It may be noted that William Morgan was several times referred to as *Mr.*, though never as *Esquire*, and it would be fair to deduce, therefore, that whatever his pretensions, he was not the head of a well-established family, neither descended from the younger son of a nobleman nor himself the son of a knight. The recently granted Blackmoor coat of arms would, no doubt, entitle the head of the household to be styled *Armiger*, and his eldest son *gent.* No doubt, too, a younger son of this household could be bullfrog enough to claim as much for himself. But in this respect a William Morgan of

Blackmoor has no advantage over any rivals we may find for him, and while it is impossible to dismiss him from all likelihood, as a possible riot-leader he hobbles badly to the fray.

Two more William Morgans, cousins, may be mentioned, difficult either to charge or discharge. Thomas Morgan of Llanfair Cilgoed and Blackbrook, Skenfrith, son of Sir Richard Morgan, the judge who condemned Lady Jane Grey to death, married Mary, daughter of Sir John Price of The Priory, Brecon. The second son of this union, William by name, married one of the Gainfords of Skenfrith but died childless. John Morgan of The Waen, Skenfrith, Sir Richard Morgan's nephew, whose altar-tomb is to be seen in Skenfrith Church, and who was both Farmer of the Duchy of Lancaster and last Governor of Skenfrith Castle, also had a second son named William who died childless, and apparently unmarried. The probability is that both these Williams were Catholic. One of them, at least, was concerned in the troubles at The Darren. As a participant there, the representative of the old Blackbrook family[4] is the more likely, because his wife was alleged to accompany him to mass: but the very fact of his association with The Darren precludes him from consideration for the vacancy at Treville. The name of 'William Morgan of Skenfrith' in the Bishop's lists was almost certainly so written to distinguish him from '*Mr.* William Morgan' of Treville Park. Morgan of The Waen died in 1608, possibly by violence at the hands of Thomas Andrew of London.[5] His single state may suggest him as a likelier rebel, but apart from the fact that it would provide a reason for the co-operation of The Darren with the Catholics of the Whitfield flock, there is no other reason for supposing that he ever lived in Treville Park.

William Morgan of Werngochyn, Llantilio Pertholey, a farm-house a mile south of the Abergavenny–Skenfrith road and no great distance from Abergavenny itself, has one point in his favour. His pedigree in *Llyfr Baglan* shows a brother of his, Walter Morgan, to have been a priest[6] and another relative, Anne, possibly Walter's natural daughter,[7] to have married Thomas

Prichard of The Grange in Campston. This last may have been the
man who made the dispositions in Treville Park on the night when
the Bishop of Hereford and Sir James Scudamore came to seize
William Morgan. The Grange apparently belonged to Dore
Abbey, which might explain why the Bishop of Hereford referred to it as in Dore parish, when in fact it was not. If Morgan
and Prichard were uncle and nephew by marriage, as well as
fellow-recusants, it would readily explain the lengths to which
Prichard was prepared to go.

This does not, however, make a strong case. It is a long way
from Werngochyn to Treville, much farther than from Skenfrith
and The Darren. No contemporary document so far seen links the
Morgans of Werngochyn with Treville. The compiler of the
pedigree, although a native of the district, was not even certain
who Anne Morgan was,[8] and any weight on her relationship with
William Morgan of Werngochyn is unwisely placed. In the circumstances the possibility of an identification here should receive
short shrift.

One hazard, and the strongest, remains. In riches, status, devotion to the Catholic cause, and turbulence, no one has a stronger
claim to the leadership of the outbreak than William Morgan of
Llantarnam, Monmouthshire. Eldest son to Edward Morgan of
Llantarnam, who had been Sheriff of Monmouthshire in 1582
while still a young man, and Member of Parliament for the
County in 1586, and his first wife, Elizabeth, daughter of Hugh
Smith of Long Ashton in Somerset,[9] William had already a considerable record officially as a troublemaker. Two years previously
he and his father, his stepmother Margery, the daughter of Hugh
Hasel, and his brother George, of Lansor Fawr, had been defendants in the Star Chamber in an action brought by Sir William
Morgan of Machen, alleging burials with popish rites, affrays
at Abergavenny, Usk and elsewhere, and other conduct
contemporaneously described as malignant recusancy. When
Queen Elizabeth's death was reported he had attempted
to seize the armour of the County of Monmouth (and

possibly that of Hereford also), for which he was again cited in the Star Chamber, though the matter was subsequently 'made upp'.

The correspondence between this activity and that outlined by the Bishop of Hereford in his allegations against William Morgan of Treville Park is very close. Of 'Mr. Morgan the younger of Lanternham' it was 'muttered that his meaninge was to have indeede taken upp Armes' at the Queen's death. *Mr*. Morgan of Treville, with John Smith and Eaton, alias North, the priest,[10] attempted at the same juncture to persuade Sir Charles Morgan to arms. Of Morgan of Llantarnam it was reported that 'Jones the Jesuite the Ffyerbrande of all, was seen in his companye'. According to Foley, North was one of Robert Jones's aliases, and if this were indeed so, the identification of William Morgan of Llantarnam with William Morgan of Treville could perhaps be clinched. Unfortunately for so clean and simple a conclusion the documents make it plain that Eaton, alias North, was an entirely separate person from Robert Jones, albeit one of his colleagues and agents.[11] William Morgan of Treville was nevertheless provenly part of the same circle of recusant operations as his namesake of Llantarnam, and the correspondence remains very close.

Unless Morgan of Llantarnam and Morgan of Treville were one and the same, there is, again, no obvious reason why the former should have been mentioned twice in the Sheriff's list of active recusants in the county of Hereford. Only one other gentleman not identifiable as a Herefordshireman is so named.[12] Llantarnam was, in all conscience, far away enough, well buttressed by Monmouth air, and not likely to trouble unduly the Sheriff of a neighbouring county.

The supposition that William Morgan of Llantarnam had a foot and more in Herefordshire is not, therefore, entirely unreasonable. He is described by Bradney as of Penrhos Ffwrdios near Caerleon, an estate at no great distance from his home. It is worth pointing out, however, that a grant made in 1609 to Henry Mynors of Treiago, Sergeant of the Carriages, of two parts of the lands of

William Morgan of Llantarnam[13] because of their owner's continued recusancy, refers only to a 'Capitall messuage called Pinros'.
Whether this was a 'saving operation' by a Catholic nominee or a
piece of individual one-upmanship there is no means of knowing.
But the 'Capitall messuage' in question may have been either that
Penrhos situated in the parish of St. Weonards, where the lands of
the Mynors already lay, or the manor of Penrhos six or seven miles
south-westward in the valley of the Trothy. Of the two the manor
is the more likely, partly because of its value in hard cash (in 1586
its rental was assessed at 47s. 5d. yearly) and partly because it may
have been land originally made over to William Morgan by The
Earl of Worcester, a suggestion the point of which will be more
apparent presently. As late as 1619 land in Penrhos parish was held
by William Sterrell, Worcester's mysterious secretary, a fact
which points to an original Somerset family holding of some size.

If Penrhos could be so identified, it would certainly establish
William Morgan of Llantarnam at the southern end of the axis of
disturbance, not far from The Darren and Llanrothal. It might also
explain, as will be seen later, the presence of Father Robert Jones
in that district. Nothing as yet, however, bridges the distance to
Treville. That Sir Charles Morgan may have granted a *pied-à-terre*
in his manor to a young man whose chances of inheriting his own
ancestral domains had long to wait[14] is the veriest guess. A vital
link in the chain is missing.

A motive for Morgan of Llantarnam's turbulence in May and
June 1605, however, is not far to seek. On April 1 previous, no
more than seven weeks before the first defiance in the churchyard
at Allensmore, Edward Morgan, the father, had appeared before
Sir Christopher Yelverton[15] and Sir David Williams, justices of
assize sitting at Usk, accused of non-attendance at Church, and had
suffered forfeiture to the Crown of two-thirds of the rents of his
lands and manors.[16] Not even the Morgans of Llantarnam, rich
as they were in secularized monastic property and replete with the
additional profit of woodlands sold for cash to the undertakers of
the Tintern wireworks,[17] could claim to be among the handful of

recusant families who under the penal legislation revived in February 1604 were opulent enough to pay the crippling fine of £20 a month. Indeed, there were in 1603, by Gardiner's calculation, no more than sixteen recusants in the country with enough of riches to face it. Smaller fry forfeited two-thirds of their lands to the Crown, whose Commissioners leased them out again for an agreed rental to courtiers and office-holders (which was the case with William's messuage of Penrhos in 1609, rented by Henry Mynors), the forfeiture to continue until such time as the owners conformed. The judgment of Usk was therefore a blow of the first consequence. The Marches of Wales, turbulent and inaccessible as they were, had, as Essex country, enjoyed some additional immunity from the worst aspects of Elizabeth's policy towards recusants. The thoroughness of the presentations by the Bishops of Llandaff and Hereford in late 1604 and early 1605 was something new. Catholic landed families which had not earlier been perplexed had suddenly to choose between a ruinous acquiescence and an active intention to resist, and William Morgan, incensed at the seizure of his still-distant patrimony, was not the man quietly to go down to poverty. To suppose that the outbreak in Herefordshire and Monmouthshire was unconnected with the dire and presumptive ruin facing Catholic landowners in the region is entirely implausible, the more so since William Morgan of Treville when in the Tower was apparently defended on these grounds and ultimately allowed to betake himself homeward.

Whether or not the concurrent Morgans are identified any the more closely by this fact, it is worth recording that on July 17, 1606 a licence was issued to Edward and William Morgan of Llantarnam, father and son, releasing them from their confinement to a circle within five miles' radius of their home and permitting them for a period of twelve months to travel 'to any place within the realm of England'. The former imposition was 'in respect of their recusancy'. But this imprecise phrase may conceal the terms on which William had been allowed to return home, namely that he reside at Llantarnam, not Treville, and refrain from visiting Abergavenny or any other place where he might encounter his former associates. No other such remission to recusants appears from the Salisbury Papers of 1606, a year of ferocious temper towards Papists as a result of the Gunpowder Plot. This in itself is odd. It was not much more than nine months since William Morgan of Treville had been haled off to London, and little more than twelve since Edward Morgan of Llantarnam had appeared in court at Usk. For unrepentant recusancy there could be in strict law no remission, and Edward Morgan's record of recusancy seems to have been unbroken. That favour could be shown to the Llantarnam family indicates some influence with the Council: it may even conceivably suggest that the arguments which made possible Morgan of Treville's release from the Tower had power to aid him further and better his terms.

It is time to say something of this influence with the Council and to make about William Morgan of Llantarnam what is the most surprising single revelation yet. He had in 1596 married Frances, fourth of the six daughters of the Earl of Worcester, thus becoming one of a select band of sons-in-law which included Sir Edward Winter of Lydney and Thomas, Lord Arundel of Wardour. The implications of this may be considerable. If Llantarnam and Treville were indeed linked, Worcester's mission into Herefordshire loses what roseate hues it has. The delicacy of the Council's initial treatment of the outbreak and their exaggeration of its dangers would be the more immediately understandable if they had learned at an early stage that Worcester's son-in-law was its instigator. Equally understandable would be the decision to send down the Earl himself, even if a cottonwool policy of this sort was bound to choke the Bishop of Hereford and the justices as well as to nonplus the rebels. These last would take their quietus readily enough from one who was their natural overlord and co-religionary, and his known relationship with their leader would explain away for them much of the essential contradiction. Again, if it should be true that William Morgan left Treville in the Bishop's custody with the mental equivalent of a smirk, and proved recalcitrant

under examination, it could well have been because Sir Roger
Bodenham had reminded him of the strength of his defenders at
Court. The obscure reference to kinship in Morgan's confession
may point in the same direction.

It will perhaps seem that this is a tallish edifice to erect on conjecture. But if it has no other result than to inspire a re-examina-
tion of the activities of the Earl of Worcester, already suggested
as curious, something will have been achieved.

There is some evidence from the Catholic side which widens
the basis of the conjecture. According to a manuscript in the hand
of Father Humphrey Evans, alias Browne (subsequently a victim
of Oates's accusations), once kept at St. Winifred's, Holywell, but
now at the Catholic Presbytery, Hornby, near Lancaster, Father
Robert Jones, zealous *operarius* and 'ffyerbrande of all', was the
priest responsible for the conversion of the Lady Frances Somerset,
William Morgan's wife. That the daughter of a man once described as a 'stiff papist' should need to be converted to the Roman
faith is perhaps matter for surprise, but as Professor A. H. Dodd
has pointed out, a dualism among Catholics at that time (which
need surprise no student of twentieth-century political systems)
made it possible to treat religious belief as a private matter which
yet permitted of full participation in the politics of Church and
State. Worcester's 'stiffness' after Elizabeth's death, has, in any
case, been much doubted, though how far justly, when all the evidence is considered, cannot here be discussed. He certainly had a
Welsh Protestant tutor for his children, which is curious enough.
But his dispositions, whether *politique* or merely lax, were scattered
like chaff before the wind of Father Robert Jones's zeal. Not for
nothing was the latter frequently resident at Llantarnam. Nor was
it surprising that he was seen in William Morgan's company.
Before long he had gained such ascendancy over the Lady Frances
that in all spiritual matters she deferred entirely to him. And
through her, according to Humphrey Evans's account, Father
Jones converted her sisters also. This last has the air of rapt
exaggeration so often generated by innocent single-mindedness,

for the Earl of Worcester's daughters, several of whom had married Catholics, were widely sundered geographically. But the pressure was there, no doubt of it.

The enthusiasm of the convert is notorious. Herself married to a lifelong Catholic and no man of straw at that, the Lady Frances was not slow in drawing attention to a certain lack of logic in her husband's procedures. 'She reflecting that most of her husband's estate consisted of Church livings, dealt with him about making some satisfaction for the same. Both her husband and herself conceived well that missionants of the Society should be maintained in both parts of Wales to labour therein, and accordingly the lady made a will, her husband assenting and subscribing thereunto, and thereby ordered that two of the Society should be maintained in North and two in South Wales for that end and purpose, but the maintenance to be allowed when the estate come into their hands, viz. after the death of her husband's father. . . .'

Whether William Morgan allowed himself a wry smile we shall never know. Uxorious he may have been, possibly his wife's equal in zeal. Even so, he was assisting in an extraordinary procedure. Few modern husbands would do as much. The wife who in 1605 felt free to pledge her husband's patrimony by a will of her own was a very exemplar of zeal and source of religious infection. Indeed, the suspicion is aroused that this account is both too simple and deliberately misleading, that pledged by the will, additionally, were the Lady Frances's own expectations, more immediate than her husband's. The Earl of Worcester's will in 1628 made no bequest to his fourth daughter,[18] and whether or not he was still 'the Earl of so small revenue and so many children' to whom Lady Russell had referred half-amusedly in 1597, one of the inferences that might be drawn from this is that she had received her share already and used it in the missionary cause dear to her heart. Certainly the Jesuit Mission in Wales, the College of St. Francis Xavier as it was called by the Vice-Provincial, was established well before 1628. Certainly, also, William Morgan never 'enjoyed' the Llantarnam lands,[19] and however the Mission was set on foot it was not with any large endowment of Llantarnam money. The cost of the Catholic establishment in Wales was *said* to have been raised by 'collections', by the putting by of alms; but recusancy continued to be a grave economic burden, and it may be wondered whether such phraseology was not a deliberate cover for a single bequest whose political implications might be dangerous.

One fact, in any case, bears heavily on this. The forfeiture by Sir Edward Morgan in April 1605 of two-thirds of his Llantarnam lands was more than a blow to family pride and the egotism of inheritance. It both cut a hole in William Morgan's pocket and overset the missionary designs so dear to his wife. Whether her will was then drawn up we do not know, but the inferences are that it was.[20] If the further supposition stands that this was William Morgan of Treville Park and this his wife a second motive for violence appears. In such case, too, Father Robert Jones may fairly be implicated. He would scarcely have been willing to see so many months of work on the Lady Frances undone by one judgment. The King's tortuous policy should rather be put to the test of force.

The thread of Catholic missionary intentions in this area may profitably be stretched a little further. Not until after the death both of the Lady Frances and of Sir Edward Morgan did Father Thomas Conway, Robert Jones's successor at Llantarnam[21] and, like him, a Flint man by birth, have opportunity to persuade William Morgan to make a grant towards the long-projected mission, and even then the endowment was objected against and endangered by William's son, Sir Edward. The important fact, however, is that at The Cwm, Llanrothal, a Jesuit training college had already been established, more than a decade earlier. Alms had been saved by Father Robert Jones, asserts the Hornby manuscript: more were saved by Father John Salisbury, who succeeded Jones in the charge of the Mission of North and South Wales,[22] until the time came when he was able to take a lease of the house of The Upper Cwm, with some land around it, for use as a Jesuit headquarters. Continued collections enabled him then in 1622 to move the Father-General for the establishment of a Jesuit College (in the sense of an official district of the Vice-Province), whose inception, by this account, was much more a matter of missionary zeal than of the bounty of 'any ... particular founder'. It may well be doubted, however, whether the recognition of Wales as the College of St. Francis Xavier by Father Blount, the first Vice-Provincial of the English Mission,[23] bears any close relationship in time to the acquisition of The Upper Cwm and the establishment of a college in the teaching sense, save that the latter certainly preceded it sufficiently to make the application by Father John Salisbury a probable success. How long before the teaching college had been populated we can only guess, but the significance of this secret Catholic focus on the Herefordshire–Monmouthshire border can hardly be exaggerated. Until its discovery at the time of the Popish Plot[24] its powerful influence rallied the waning forces of Catholicism in the Marches of Wales. Llanrothal was Little Rome long after the rest of the ecclesiastical landscape had been lost in the advance of Hun and Vandal.

The College at The Upper Cwm, whenever founded, sets two question-marks against the year 1605 in particular. The first is this: on the flyleaf of two of the books seized from the College in 1678 and now kept in the Upper Cloister Library of the Cathedral in Hereford, is the inscription '*Liber Edward Poyntz 1605. Potiora spero.*' Poyntz was then of Treget, Llanrothal, but earlier of Tobington Park in Gloucestershire, a younger brother of Sir John Poyntz of Iron Acton in that county. He was accounted one of the principal and most dangerous recusants in the diocese and 'altogether jesuited'. If this last is true, what is the significance of the inscription? '*1605. Potiora spero.*' To what does it point? Regret at the failure of the Gunpowder Plot? Not if Jesuit protestations and instructions have any validity. Mourning for the failure of William Morgan? Poyntz was not involved. May it be that 1605 represents the date of the owner's gift of the book, rather than his receipt of it, that The Cwm had even then the beginnings of a library? Had the seed indeed been sown so early and did the watchers expect its appearance with power?

The second question treads hard on the heels of the first. On whose land was The Upper Cwm, Llanrothal, situate? The answer gives suspicion nothing less than a warren to work in. *The land of the Earl of Worcester.* According to the account in the Hornby manuscript, it was Father John Salisbury who first took a lease of The Upper Cwm, and if this be true, we might infer that the College was not established before 1615. There is nothing inevitable, however, about such an inference: William Griffiths was the previous tenant, and the fact that Father Robert Jones was frequently reported in the vicinity would have made entirely possible the increasing use of The Upper Cwm as a lodging for priests, a place where books were available and intruders unlikely. If the house was so used for a number of years, the lease to Father Salisbury in 1615 may have been no more than an indication that the nucleus of a College was already in being and the risk involved in a direct lease small enough, ten years after the Powder Plot, to make subterfuge unnecessary.

In any case Worcester could hardly not have known about the lease. When Father Charles Browne, some time after 1625, paid the sum necessary to take it over from his predecessor, he also bought outright The Lower Cwm and an adjoining farm called Langunvill. Only after the Earl's death in 1628 were the lands of the College itself let with more caution, not direct to a priest, but to a layman prepared to act as a cover agent for the College.[25] Until that year the personal influence and virtual immunity of Worcester had evidently been sufficient to keep away prying eyes. The Hornby manuscript, then, is perhaps advisedly vague in its early dates. To admit the founding of a Jesuit College too near to 1605 might have unpleasant implications.

The last concern of inquiry is with the Earl himself. What were the motives of a nobleman who with high sentence first hushed a Catholic rebellion and then, how much later is not known, was instrumental in founding a Jesuit College? Not that there is anything irreconcilable in these two facts. Indeed, he doubtless believed the seeming contradiction necessary. Only a courtier, a

G

sounding-board for the King, could know enough and in time to advise and protect the recusancy of the provinces. The Earl of Worcester, then, no longer fits the shape of the venal and vapid Catholic assigned to him by several historians. His suppression of William Morgan's insurrection may have been a sham to shield a son-in-law (or alternatively, any Catholic or Catholics). It may also have been the much more genuine action of a secret follower of the Jesuits who considered the outbreak misguided or worse. In either case the mask of this tilter before royalty needs to be snatched off.

NOTES

[1] Pub. Catholic Record Society, Vol. II, p. 290.

[2] Clark, op. cit., p. 258, gives Gamul, but credits a fourth son of the match with the name of Garnons. Bradney, op. cit., p. 278, gives Garnons, but is unable to identify a Garnons Morgan whom he places tentatively in the second generation. *Llyfr Baglan* gives Garnest, but like Clark makes *Garnons* Morgan a fourth son. Almost certainly Garnons is the correct version. It was found in the locality then and still is.

[3] A William Morgan, gent., of Blackmoor died in 1660. Robinson, op. cit., p. 3. This, however, would make him too young to have been a leader in 1605.

[4] Blackbrook itself was at this time held either by Thomas Bodenham or by his niece Anne and her husband George Scudamore of Llangarren. Bradney, op. cit., Vol. II, Pt. I, p. 128.

[5] *S.P.* 38/9, *xx die Aprilis 1608*. A Pardon graunted to Thomas Andrew late of London gent for manslaughter committed upon Wm. Morgan.

[6] Op. cit., p. 69. William and Walter were second and third sons respectively to William Morgan of Werngochyn and Kateryn, daughter of George Kemes of Kemes. William's wife was Elizabeth, daughter of Roger Morgan of The Garn in Tredynog.

[7] Ibid. The compiler wrote the name of Anne Morgan under that of Walter, without inserting the conventional line of parentage.

[8] The insertion of the name of Anne under that of Walter the priest could be simply a matter of space, the expression of the compiler's belief that she *was* a member of the Werngochyn family, though he was uncertain of her relationship. As a member of a younger generation, she could be fitted in most easily to the gap caused by Walter's celibacy.

[9] Bradney, op. cit., Vol. III, Pt. II, p. 231. Another William Morgan was a half-brother by Edward Morgan's second wife.

[10] *S.P.* 14, Vol. XIV, 52. It is perhaps significant that North allegedly hurried from Monmouthshire to Herefordshire on the news of the Queen's death, saying that the Catholics were in arms in the county from which he had come. The same tactic was tried by the priest Lister, alias Butler, proceeding from Herefordshire to Worcestershire. If North came from Monmouthshire to Arkston, may not his alleged companions have done so too?

[11] *S.P.* 14, Vol. XIV, 40. Jones, Lister and Oldcorne are listed as Jesuits: 'Parrie als Williams, James Morreys als Jones, Eton als North' are 'persons likewise that are the Jesuites instruments and Priests by their calling'.

[12] Sir Francis Lacon, a native of Lancashire, included presumably because of his relationship with the Bodenhams.

[13] *S.P.* 38/9, *Docquet 2 Novembris 1609.* This Morgan is not here referred to positively as of Llantarnam, but the County and the reference to 'the revercon of certaine Mannors' after the decease of his father make it practically certain that he is intended.

[14] Edward Morgan, William's father, lived till March 1633.

[15] Of Norfolk. Created Knight at Whitehall on July 23, 1603, before the Coronation of the King. Judge of the King's Bench and, according to John Gerard the Jesuit, 'one of the leaders of the Calvinist party in England today' (*John Gerard*, p. 18).

[16] Exchequer Bills and Answers, Jac. I, Monmouth No. 70, cited by Bradney, op. cit., Vol. III, Pt. II, p. 230. Exchequer Bill, Monmouth No. 70 is concerned with the Manor of Wensland and Bryngwyn, part of the property seized from Edward Morgan in 1605. It appears from the defendants' answers that Edward Morgan had by November 1613 compounded with the Crown and re-obtained possession of the whole of the manor. *Vide Exchequer Proceedings Concerning Wales in tempore James I*, p. 257.

[17] William Morgan, grandfather of the defendant of 1605, had purchased the secularized property of the Abbey of Llantarnam in 1561 from the Earl of Pembroke. In 1575 John Wheler, partner with Andrew Palmer in the Tintern wireworks, bought Kemeys Commander wood from off the Llantarnam lands.

[18] Of six daughters she was one of two who did not benefit. Bradney, op. cit. II, pp. 14-15.

[19] According to Foley, op. cit., Vol. IV, p. 334, William Morgan lived less than a year after the death of his father, and difficulties arose not because of any unwillingness of his but because the shortness of the interval before his own death allowed him to do no more than bind his son Sir Edward, already a consenting party, to carry out his mother's will. Bradney, op. cit., Vol. III, Pt. II, p. 231, however makes William die on March 9, 1633/4 and his father on the 26th of the same month. It seems most likely either that Bradney has miscalculated the date of Edward Morgan's death by one year, or that a misprint has occurred. March 26, 1633/4 [*sic*] cannot be correct: probably it should read March 26, 1633.

[20] The will was said to have been made 'soon after her conversion' (Foley, op. cit., Vol. IV, p. 331) and since Father Jones was reported at Llantarnam

throughout 1604 (*S.P.* 14, Vol. XIV, 40), and may well have been so even earlier, it seems reasonable to suppose that the will was earlier than May 1605.

[21] I.e. in the spiritual guidance of the Lady Frances, but not in the organization of the prospective South Wales province.

[22] He was usually resident with Lady Worcester at Raglan. William Vaughan of Llangyndeyrn in July 1602 described him in a bitter warning letter to the Archbishop of Canterbury and others as 'of Denbighshire . . . yellow-headed, sanguine, and short of stature, about the age of 26, and never will have a beard'. In 1615, therefore, when Robert Jones died, he was barely in middle age. *Cal. of Salis. MSS.*, Pt. XII, p. 212.

[23] The English Mission S.J. had been created a Vice-Province by Father-General Vitelleschi in 1619 and the College of St. Francis Xavier was one of the first three Colleges of the new Vice-Province. The others were St. Ignatius (the London area) and St. Aloysius (the Lancashire region). Foley, op. cit., IV, p. 333.

[24] The exposure of the College was coupled with the seizure of Fathers Kemble and Lewis, two Monmouthshire priests both subsequently martyred. Anti-Catholic activity was directed by Bishop Herbert Croft of Hereford, an ex-Catholic and grandson of the Sir Herbert Croft of 1605, and carried out with enthusiasm by Captain James Scudamore. *A Short Narrative of the Discovery of a College of Jesuits at a Place called the Come.*

[25] To William Morton in 1637, on a 99 years' lease: subsequently to Robert Hutton, merchant, of London. *A Short Narrative of the Discovery*, p. 2. Trans. Woolhope Society, 1900, p. 14, however, refers to a deed dated November 10, 1637, by which The Cwm was leased by the Earl of Worcester to Father William Morgan. Frequent references to this Morgan subsequently show him to have been Principal of the College, and it may well be that the name Morton was introduced in error.

CHAPTER VIII

The Significance of the Outbreak

It is not pretended that the last chapter arrived at an answer that could be called *convincing*. The search for the motives which broke in such summer violence must, therefore, of necessity be inconclusive, since William Morgan is partly out of the net. In any case, reasons for the outbreak, in the most obvious sense, need not be looked for. The persecution of recusants was a very real and infuriating fact, which a perusal of Lingard[1] or any honest Protestant source[2] will at once establish. The pains and disabilities which Catholics suffered in 1605 had induced, in areas where recusancy was common and particularly in those which until a short time before were protected from its worst effects, the kind of militant resentment which made an outbreak likely, if not inevitable. These pains were none the less real because they are not considered here. The question which this chapter must discuss is not so much *Why did Catholics rebel?* as *Why these Catholics?* If no simple answer is forthcoming, at least the inquiry may provide a reading or two for the climate of Catholic opinion in the Marches and establish a gauge sensitive to dissentient airs.

The first point to engage attention is the fact that there exist *two* lists of recusants in the county of Hereford which may be assigned to Christmas 1604 or earlier. The first, and much the shorter of the two, which is found among the State Papers,[3] contains the names of those who are 'jesuited'. This list was endorsed in pencil, by a later hand, 'about June 1605', but its tone of apprehension about Spain, and its seeming ignorance of any of the happenings of Whitsun 1605, suggest that it was compiled before the Peace Treaty of 1604. Whoever compiled it believed that 'except good order bee taken in tyme, the Recusantes by the Jesuits persuasions will take upp Armes against the Kinge'. After naming the Jesuit priests at work and the seminary priests who were their instruments, he commented that 'All these persons have nothing in their mouthes but the sworde the sworde [*sic*] and warres. . . .' It was Jesuit belief at the time of writing, he alleged, that the death of the late Queen had benefited them not at all: they were 'leapt out of the fryeing panne into the fier'. As well try their strength therefore. 'They bragg much that they shall have Assistance from the Kinge of Fraunce and the Kinge of Spayne. In respect of which persuasions many Catholicks in Wales are in greate feare and doe wishe the Jesuits with all their adherents out of the Land.'

There are Catholic writers of recent years who have been concerned to deny the nature and the strength of the differences among practising Catholics in 1605 and earlier and to imply that those who did not share Jesuit preparedness to use either foreign influence or force or both were to that extent false to their religious faith. Father Philip Caraman in his Introduction to *John Gerard*,[4] for instance, does not hesitate to assert that when Gerard, whose zeal both as Jesuit and Catholic is beyond doubt, referred to the Archpriest Controversy (namely, the appeal to Rome made in 1600 by the secular clergy against the appointment as Archpriest of George Blackwell, a Jesuit nominee), as a quarrel between the Jesuits and a 'group of restless priests' he was 'making a distinction between the great body of secular clergy and a mischief-making clique'. The leaders of this clique, he goes on, probably hitting at Dr. Owen Lewis, Bishop of Cassano, were often in comfortable exile: some of its members in Britain lived under safe-conducts or had been driven by circumstances and deficiencies of character, as with William Watson, to apostacy: all, he says, were prepared to come to an understanding with the Government without the guarantees which true recusancy demanded, namely, that the conscience of Catholics should be respected, that they should be excused attendance at Protestant services, and that they should be allowed both limited facilities to attend Mass and to educate their children as they wished.

It is difficult to see what service an analysis of this sort does either to history or to the Catholic religion. That the Jesuits were successful in the end in defeating their rivals abroad and in obtaining from Rome retrospective recognition of the correctness both of their policy and conduct has little reference either to a moral issue or to the balance of opinion among Catholics in England in 1605. If Dr. Owen Lewis was 'comfortable', was Father Parsons, the Society's chief engineer, any less? Wales, in particular, would have rejected with some violence at this time any attempt by the Jesuited party to represent themselves as the unique repository of zeal and wisdom. W. Llywelyn Williams pointed out,[5] as long as sixty years ago, that almost every Welsh Catholic of consequence on the Continent in the latter half of the sixteenth century – Morris Clynog, Hugh Griffith, Rhosier Smith, Owen Lewis, Thomas Morgan, John and Edward Bennett – was ranked amongst the opponents of the Jesuits. In Britain itself the Bennett brothers, Roger Cadwallader and Jonas Meredith (the last-named Bristol-born though doubtless of Welsh extraction) were concerned either in the Wisbech Stirs or as appellants in the Archpriest controversy. Other Welsh Catholics of some eminence, like David Baker, evidently preferred to revive and give status to the Benedictine Order rather than associate themselves with the Jesuits. It is probably not without significance, either, that some at least of Robert Jones's supporting priests in the College of St. Francis Xavier had to be Englishmen, and that many of his lay supporters were incomers from England. No, the verdict of history, if it had fallen to Welshmen to give it, would certainly not have gone to the Society. The ejection of the Welsh party from the English College at Rome had had wide and continuing repercussions.

That the Jesuits, again, as the party of militancy, were able to point out among the Catholic moderates a proportion of faint-hearts, a fringe of unstable egoists and fools, is a political commonplace. Fanaticism can usually attach to itself a monopoly of sincerity and self-denial. But that *all* the *English* party among the Catholics were prepared to accept an understanding with the Government without sufficient guarantees of freedom of conscience may be dismissed as plainly and simply untrue. This political shadow which the Jesuits even now attempt to cast over the history of Catholicism leaves as unjust a picture of the religious sincerity of the *English* wing of the Catholics of James's reign as does Professor Trevor-Roper's determination to deny to the Jesuits any political or patriotic virtue, indeed any moral standing, by using as his shibboleth the fact that England and Spain were (until 1604) at war.[6]

There are, in truth, two questions at issue: first, the degree of religious enthusiasm, what may be called the zeal for the continuance of Catholic worship and belief, which the Jesuits and the English party might respectively claim: second, the views held by the rival groups as to the means by which such continuance might best be achieved, the English party being content with toleration, being Englishmen first and Catholics second, and the Jesuits still hankering after Counter-Reformation, to be achieved, if necessary, by the military victory of a foreign power. The chances that ability and fanatical enthusiasm would be found among the few, and those in the Jesuit camp, are, of course, high: the Society's methods of selection alone would ensure that. It is also probable that among the English party must be numbered the venal and the faltering, the potential turncoats and the infirm of purpose. But at a time of genuine persecution these were by no means so many as fanaticism would suggest. Moreover, Jesuit arrogance, and, in the case of Welshmen, Jesuit affronts to national feeling, had forced into the opposite Catholic wing a number of priests of ability and devotion. There were not a few, even then, who resented a monopoly both of pastoral virtue and political wisdom.

To try to estimate religious zeal, however, by applying a particular view of political means, remains a barren exercise. It is impossible not to agree with Professor Trevor-Roper, nevertheless, that the Jesuits repeatedly show signs, both now and in the reigns of Elizabeth and James, of wishing to have the record in their favour even when the facts are not.

The conditions for an understanding with the Government which Father Caraman suggests were fundamental to the maintenance of a sincere Catholicism were, it should be noted, the very ones on which Roger Cadwallader and his associates made an unsuccessful attempt to negotiate in January 1603.[7] Their refusal to surrender themselves when the terms were not honoured, despite Archbishop Bancroft's cozenings, suggests that they were no less zealous in a religious sense than were the Jesuits, and that the differences between the two wings of Catholic opinion were almost entirely the product of widely-separated political attitudes. It would be interesting to know for what Cadwallader was martyred in 1610, if not for the continuous, active and defiant exercise of his function as a Catholic priest.

The pretensions of the Society to a monopoly of zeal and martyrdom could not allow that he should die unreconciled to their political position, the more since Cadwallader eight times on the steps of the scaffold refused the Oath of Supremacy[8] and engaging all the Catholics present to join with him in prayer, which they audibly and publicly did,[9] made a particularly brave and moving end. It was an answer from the English party which was bound to be heard along the whole of the Southern March. Father Robert Jones thereupon put out an account of his death which, while giving him full credit for constancy of spirit and courage, was concerned to let it be known that while in prison he had declared himself (to a Jesuit priest unnamed) completely purged of all his enmity against the Society, in mark of which he presented to that same priest his entire personal library. Father Jones himself contrived to visit him in prison on the day that sentence of death was pronounced,[10] but added no details, on his own authority, of the alleged reconciliation. It is significant that there is in existence a Latin manuscript signed 'Dentor' which denies absolutely both

Cadwallader's reconciliation to the Society of Jesus and his gift of books. There continued, evidently, a war to which the Protestant Government was an uncomprehending third party.

Some enlargement upon the subject of divisions among Catholics has been necessary not merely because south-west Herefordshire might reasonably be expected to reflect the nearness and influence of Wales but because it was indubitably an area in which the ministrations of Robert Jones were in immediate juxtaposition, if not opposition, to those of Roger Cadwallader. The high proportion of 'incomers' in the Herefordshire list of persons 'jesuited' (compiled in 1604 or earlier) is therefore a point to engage attention. But it would be unwise to conclude too readily either that the tendency to jesuitry increased with the degree of anglicization or that the absence of the jesuited party from the outbreak of 1605 can be explained by the fact that many of them, having no lands to speak of (and being, in some instances, elderly folk who had come to enjoy the practice of their religion without interruption) were not likely to be incensed by the new confiscations. The problem is not so simple as to admit of such generalized conclusions. What has to be faced is that, although the compiler of the 1604 list believed that it was from among the Jesuits and their followers that armed rebellion was seriously to be expected, only three of the persons named in that category (if we agree William Morgan to be of Llantarnam) had any part in the disturbances following the death of Alice Wellington. Moreover, Dr. Harley, one of the three, seems to have been a messenger bringing warning to Treville Park, possibly even a warning to forbear. The part of James Morris, alias Jones, the seminary priest, one of the 'instruments ... who at the Jesuits assignment doe very much hurt',[11] is more difficult to determine and must be considered later.

What conclusions may fairly be drawn from the absence of the 'jesuited' party from among those implicated in the outbreak? Not all of them were incomers, in any recent sense, and not all unlanded. Many perhaps, although resident in the county, were too far away. But what of Edward Poyntz of Treget, William

Griffiths of The Cwm and Bonner of Llanrothal, all three close to one of the two centres of disturbance?[12] Above all why no hue, no cry, why not so much as a whisper, after Father Robert Jones, reputedly *the ffyerbrande of all?*[13] He may, of course, have been at the farthest confine of his mission at the time of the outbreak, but a period of violence covering six weeks afforded him ample opportunity to return. The silence surrounding him can hardly be without significance. Undoubtedly the simplest conclusion to reach is that the disorders of Whitsun 1605 were the expression of individual grievances and were begun in ignorant miscalculation of the consequences: they were quite unplanned by the Jesuit cadre in the district, whose attitude may even have been one of hostility to the encouragers of such folly.

Such few facts as are known about the intentions of the rebels must be set out. A state of militancy evidently existed before Whitsun because Roger Cadwallader had drawn up and dispatched to the justices a manifesto, of which William Morgan was able to plead ignorance. If Morgan himself were of Llantarnam, the probable cause of militancy in his case would have been the Court decision of April 1, by which two-thirds of the family lands stood forfeit. But the effect was more general than this. The thoroughness of the recent presentations had frightened Catholics high and low and, with or without Cadwallader's participation, William Morgan and his group meant to try a little violence as an antidote to episcopal activity. The funeral of Alice Wellington, intended primarily as a demonstration of defiance, provided an opportunity for further action for which the Catholics of Allensmore and Hungerstone were not entirely unprepared. The rescue of Leonard Marsh was improvised, but battle temper was about the coverts days before it.

An additional factor appears in the arrival of James Morris, alias Jones, bringing his own supply of gall. The letter he wrote to Father Cresswell in Madrid and sent by David Butler was, according to the Earl of Salisbury, 'full of poison' and its author 'well worth the apprehension'.[14] He had also written two letters to gentlemen[15] at Court and proposed to journey to London himself to solicit a change of policy towards Catholics.[16] Plainly, therefore, the militancy in the neighbourhood of Treville and Allensmore was to be accompanied by the pressure of advocacy in London, a two-point plan which probably seemed the more likely to succeed because of Rice Griffiths's assurance that the Bishop of Hereford's firmness would not be backed by the Archbishop.

There are two main difficulties about the simple acceptance of this picture. The first is caused by the uncertain identity of William Morgan, already discussed at length, the second by the record and affiliations of James Morris, alias Jones. These difficulties must now be analysed.

The reserve of the gentry influenced by the Jesuits makes it as plain as can be that William Morgan was counselled mainly by Roger Cadwallader and aided by men of lowly birth like James Coles and the Marsh brothers. If he was a gentleman in anything more than a minor sense, then he was virtually alone in taking up violence, working off his spleen behind a company so short of breeding that William Mynors of Oldfield,[17] a cadet of the Treiago family, appeared in it heroically tall. But if he was William Morgan of Llantarnam there is the additional gap, not merely between Llantarnam and Treville, but between a man counselled by Father Robert Jones and one counselled by Roger Cadwallader. It was not till July 1605, and as a result of the turbulence at Allensmore, Treville and The Darren, that Henry Garnet, Superior of the English Province of the Society of Jesus, wrote to Rome for a papal brief condemning Catholics who rose in arms.[18] Meanwhile somebody – and need we doubt that it was Robert Jones? – was telling the gentry of the region to have nothing to do with the outbreak. Why should William Morgan of Llantarnam, so deeply pledged already to Jesuit plans for the Welsh mission, be suddenly free of them all and attentive to a man of known hostility to the Jesuits? No single argument makes so difficult as does this a belief in Treville as Llantarnam Parva.

Yet any one argument can weigh too heavily. If William Morgan of Llantarnam, whatever the confiscations he had suffered, can scarcely be envisaged as leaving 'the ffyerbrande of all' to find a bellows elsewhere, it must be remembered that the documented career of William Morgan – any William Morgan, whether of Blackmoor, Kilpeck, Werngochyn or The Waen – is scarcely less contradictory. When he attempted to persuade Sir Charles Morgan in 1603 to take up arms he was under the influence of Reginald Eaton, alias North, one of Robert Jones's 'instruments', and was presumably intending to resist the accession of James I in favour of the Infanta of Spain. Later the same year he was reputedly associated with Cadwallader in Watson's Plot, an enterprise reserved for the wilder fringe of the *English party*. In 1605 he was again in arms, counselled immediately perhaps by James Morris, alias Jones, but not far from the ministrations of Cadwallader, which he regularly attended. Such a contradictory record reveals this William Morgan, whoever he was, as a natural turbulent, a man of confused thinking whose impulses to action answered the pressures of Church and Council as swiftly as a counter-punch. Perhaps it is of little moment to seek to make of him either Jesuit or anti-Jesuit, whatever the alignments farther back.

To speculate briefly on the identity of Francis Foster, the man who was seized in William Morgan's house, may not, however, be without profit in discovering the point of view of the conspirators. He appears, in the first place, in the list of *sojourners* in the county. From a variety of documents he can be more fully described as Francis Foster, alias Bishop, of Warwickshire. His curious position as a guest of William Morgan's over a considerable period[19] suggests that he was a priest. It is not impossible that he was one and the same with Francis Foster, a younger son of Thomas Foster of Tonge, Co. Salop, and his wife, who was born Ursula Vyse of Staunton, Staffordshire, and died as a recusant in 1590 in Shrewsbury Gaol.[20] This Francis was admitted in 1592 to the English College at Rome and was one of six students dismissed in 1597, presumably in the disturbance immediately preceding the appointment of Father Parsons as Rector for the second time. If this was the 'sojourner' at Treville, he could hardly have been other than an anti-Jesuit, a disciple of Richard Powell and John Bennett who reputedly 'curbed' Parsons and complained to the Cardinals of the misgovernment of the College.[21] A man, indeed, after the heart of Roger Cadwallader. The one-time student at Rome was finally ordained priest from the English College at Douai and sent to the English mission in 1598. Thereafter little seems to be known of his movements, save that after a time he was caught, sent to Newgate, and banished in 1606. Nothing in this record is inconsistent with the part of Foster, alias Bishop, at Treville, which may well have been the place of his apprehension. The subsequent admission of Foster the seminary priest into the Benedictine Order, revived in 1607 mainly by the efforts of David Baker of Abergavenny and Leander Jones of Llanfrynach, Breconshire, both confirms his anti-Jesuit sympathies and suggests contact, from college days in Rome onwards, with the Welsh party among the priesthood.

Surmise much of this must be. Yet an unidentified William Morgan, albeit of some standing, counselled by Cadwallader and Foster and followed with pugnacity by James Coles, Cadwallader's massing clerk, the Marsh brothers and other artisans from the neighbourhood, is the centre of a unified picture. It is a picture, of course, largely created by William Morgan's 'confession', and one may wonder just why there appear in it Sais of Withington and William Mynors of Oldfield, neither of whom can be identified positively with any of the acts of riot and defiance, while Philip Giles, Thomas Prichard, Rice ap Rice and Thomas Quarrell, all of higher rank than Coles and the Marsh brothers and participants of some determination, were not mentioned at all as having 'had speech' with their leader.

The same query arises about the man who presents the second and much greater difficulty in explaining the outbreak, James Morris, alias Jones. For he was William Morgan's scapegoat. It was James Jones, Morgan would have it, who came to his house 'out of monmouthe shiere', James Jones who adjured Cole,

Leonard Marsh, Foster and himself that they should strike before the Bishop of Hereford, who 'ment to take some hard course' with them, and James Jones again who not only wrote two letters to London but promised, with Morgan himself, to go up there to persuade certain influential persons to intercede on behalf of the Catholics. It was Jones, furthermore, who had organized a subscription among the Catholics thereabouts, Morgan went on, and had had enough of the proceeds about him to reward John Mynors, his messenger to London, with ten shillings.

If this account should prove false or greatly exaggerated, then William Morgan's motives in giving it were probably to exculpate as far as possible Roger Cadwallader, about whom he was more than vague, and Rice Griffiths, whom he mentioned only as an influence in high places. On the other hand, its falseness could have been simply a recognition of the Council's possession of Jones's letters, and of the fact that he was safely away and in hiding. The difficulty becomes much more acute if it be assumed that William Morgan ground out a recognizable version of the truth, and it will be necessary now to examine that difficulty in some detail.

While it may yet come to proof that Whitfield was held and occupied by the Vaughans of Llanrothal (as heirs of John Gwillim of Cillwch), the most obvious reason for the solidarity of the recusants at The Darren with those of Treville is supplied by the presence in both areas of James Morris, alias Jones. But in 1604 he had been described as 'an instrument' of the Jesuits. In 1605 the Jesuits and their lay followers among the gentry lay close and quiet. What had happened to create this contradiction? In the middle Monnow valley the Jesuit abstinence is demonstrable in a way impossible at Treville. The Darren, at which James Jones ministered, was no more than a mile and a half distant from The Cwm, at which Fathers Jones and Powell might be found. But where, even if there were *no* Jesuit priest in the vicinity, were the embattled Griffithses of Penmark when the 'fighting masses' at The Darren were celebrated, masses faithfully attended by the Morgans of Skenfrith and the entire household of William Vaughan of Llanrothal? There may have been some discrepancy of social status between those who looked to The Cwm and those at The Darren: the Morgans of The Waen and Vaughans of Llanrothal apart, those who met at the hamlet upstream have the look of cottagers. But this is not enough for explanation: James Morris, alias Jones, it must appear, had some grievance, some personal cause for baleful oratory, which was strong enough both to defy his mentors and to rally his congregation at The Darren to his cause. But the better-advised gentry made no move. Despite the possibility that Rice Griffiths was a frequent visitor at the house of Sir Charles Morgan's mother,[22] nothing incontrovertible connects the family of Griffiths of Penmark with the actual outbreak. The silence surrounding them is as impenetrable as that round Father Robert Jones.

Of what cause James Morris, alias Jones, had for his sudden inflammation there is no sign. Bitterness such as William Morgan attributed to his visitor could have been the immediate result of a recent quarrel between The Darren and The Cwm, and it is likely from the sequence of events that James Jones returned first to his congregation to rally and instruct them before he went up to London.[23] That there was a grievance which this man deliberately espoused is certainly suggested both from the tone of the captured letters and also from the fact that he intended to explain himself to Father Joseph Cresswell in Madrid. James Jones, it may reasonably be surmised, had had a violent difference of opinion with his Jesuit superiors over tactics, and was bidding for support abroad over the head of Father Robert Jones. For the party of militancy to counsel caution, while their supposedly lukewarm rivals were heating threat into riot, must, after all, have troubled many a habitual enthusiast.

It is possible, too, that James Jones was not alone in his revolt. That David Butler who in July slipped out of Cardiff on board *The Speedwell* could have been one of his colleagues. Butler was an alias of Thomas Lister the Jesuit, reputedly a worker in

Herefordshire and often resident at Bromyard with the Abingtons. Lister was a propagandist in the Jesuit cause[24] who had earned himself an extreme of odium among the secular clergy at the time of the Archpriest controversy by the publication of his *Treatise on Schism*,[25] a pamphlet which itself became the first of the six grounds of the appeal by thirty-three priests in November 1600 against George Blackwell. In this work his headlong and public invective had put even Father Henry Garnet, his Superior, who earlier had entertained grave doubts about his prudence, in no little difficulty.[26] In May 1601 Lister's *Treatise* was suppressed by papal brief, but the brief was delayed by the Archpriest till January 1602. His hotheadedness had not gone entirely unappreciated.

For William Watson, an opponent of equal weight, Thomas Lister had offered an admirable mark. His studies for his doctor's cap, wrote Watson in his *Quodlibets*, 'being as it seemed above his capacity, made his brains idle, his wits flie out, and his head light ever after'.[27] Reputedly associated with Lister in this sterile controversy had been both Father Cresswell and Father Robert Jones.[28]

There is no known reason of time and geography why Lister should not have been in the vicinity. When he first came to England in 1596 he was lodged at Hindlip Castle, Worcestershire, with the Abingtons, and though at a later stage Hampshire was his hiding-place,[29] from 1603 onwards he was reported as working in Worcestershire and Herefordshire. At Queen Elizabeth's death, together with Eaton, alias North, he made a vigorous attempt to rouse the Catholics of the Southern Marches to arms. His association with the group at The Cwm is not in doubt. A man of violent impulse, who was for long kept from the degree of responsibility in the Society which his abilities merited,[30] he could very well have joined James Jones in objecting to the inaction counselled by Father Robert Jones and in seeking to persuade the Jesuit hierarchy abroad that opportunities were being missed. Admittedly the attitude of Butler's captors does not suggest that in the pseudo-merchant

H

they recognized priest,[31] but Thomas Lister was in fact captured in 1605, at a time unknown, committed to prison and banished in the following year. It is not impossible, therefore, that it was at Cardiff he was seized.

James Jones the priest and his part in the outbreak loose one last arrow-flight, perhaps of fancy. In the *Salisbury Papers* of 1606 a breviat of the confession of George Charnock, then a prisoner in Worcester Gaol under accusation of complicity in the attempted escape of the Gunpowder Plotters Robert Winter and Stephen Littleton (whom Charnock was to have guided from Hagley, Worcestershire, to The Cwm), includes the following words: 'He says that Jones the priest and his son sometimes use the house of Mrs. Griffith of Combe . . .'[32] *His son!* To whom does this point save James Morris, alias Jones?—James Jones the widower with many children who in his late twenties went overseas and took orders?[33] Fancy this may be, but it could go some way to explain the link between a riot in Cadwallader's country and armed masses in the Jesuit domain of the middle Monnow at a time when no general command to rebellion was either given or favoured by the Jesuit hierarchy. That James Jones was temporarily incensed at the Stuart régime Chief Justice Popham's account of his letters suggests. If his insensate action allowed him both to inflame William Morgan and yet to carry with him Lister, this may have been possible only because of his peculiar relationship with Father Robert Jones.

It is time now to examine the nature of the *post hoc* explanations of the outbreak. The Council's propagandists were first in the field. *The Late Commotion of Certaine Papists in Herefordshire*, published in 1605 on some date unknown (but presumably before November),[34] purported to be an exchange of letters between one Thomas Hamond, who took upon himself to publish them 'to stop the mouths of the multitude', and his friend Mr. E. R. of Hereford. The latter's account is, at least in appearance, strictly factual. It begins with the burial of Alice Wellington and with some skill takes the story as far as the rescue of Leonard Marsh, adding a dutiful postscript about the arrival of the Earl of Worces-

ter. Hamond himself attacks the reader with a digest of the Lord
Chancellor's Star Chamber speech of June 20, which blamed the
outbreak upon the laxity of the justices of the peace, whose attitude had given full echo to priestly whisperings 'that the tymes are
like to alter'. The point of the pamphlet, apart from the alarm
which the details of Catholic violence would touch off among
Protestants at a distance, appears to have been twofold: it was both
an apologia for the royal policy and a proclamation of the current
royal attitude, full of threatening probabilities for recusancy. King
James, by this account, found 'there was no more perfit forme of
government in the world, nor any Church that came so neere
unto the very substance of the trueth in every poynt, as the Church
of England doth'.[35] He was not, in fact, for swapping horses.[36] Nor
was there any prospect of toleration.

No attempt was made to examine the causes of the commotion.
It was sufficient to name malignant recusancy and threaten it for
the future. Indeed, any explanation which did more than set out
the violence might well become more of an embarrassment to the
Council than a propaganda point.

Factually correct or not, *The Late Commotion* was an account
superficial. It neither sought nor provided reasons. Catholic confessions and interpretations, despite their variety, reveal little more.
William Morgan in his *confession* implied that he had foreknowledge that the Bishop 'ment to take some hard course' with
Catholics and admitted that he was advised by James Jones to get a
blow in first. This was the answer most likely to appeal to the
equivocal attitude behind the Council's stern front, and allowed
apologists to attack the Bishop as a bungler. If William Morgan
had indeed influence in high places and had been advised of the
balance of feeling at Court, his confessed motive may have had
little reference to truth.

At the examination of Rice Griffiths by the Bishop of Hereford
and Paul Delahay, Lewis Watkins of Kivernoll and William Caunt
of Madley, the latter of whom had been present at every scene of
violence in the Allensmore district from the burial of Alice

Wellington onwards, deposed that the prisoner had encouraged
the rioters by promising them immunity. The Archbishop of
Canterbury, he had claimed, had persuaded the King that the
commotion was a matter of a broken head or two, no more, and
that those who thought otherwise would not be listened to.[37]
Griffiths was indeed to be cast for the part of *agent provocateur* in
subsequent versions. Ignorance and treacherous incitement were
to be the main planks of the Catholic defence.

Father Robert Parsons, in his pamphlet *A Treatise tending to
Mitigation*, published in 1607, but written in 1606, as the phrase
used of Hamond's pamphlet, 'set forth the yeare past', indicates,
very justly declared that the main purpose of *The Late Commotion*
was, by the reprinting of the sermon of the Bishop of London at
St. Paul's Cross on August 5 and the charge to the Judges given by
the Lord Chancellor in the Star Chamber, to threaten Catholics
further and to disabuse them publicly of all hopes of better treatment.[38] The Allensmore incident, he wrote, was the work only of
'a few poore countrey people Catholickly affected', who did what
they did solely to prevent a corpse from rotting above ground.
Exaggeration above measure had followed, by book, sermon and
speech, till 'Catholics generally were most odiously traduced'.[39]

To complain of the increasing bitterness of the Catholic lot was,
indeed, Father Parsons's main intention.

> 'No man endeavoureth to mollify matters, but all to exas-
> perate: no man applieth lenitives, but all corrosives; no man
> powreth in wyne or oyle into the wound, but all salte and
> vinegar; . . . all cry and clap their hands to exulceration, saying
> with the children of Edom, in the day of Hierusalems affliction:
> *Exinanite, exinanite, usque ad fundamentum in ea*'.[40]

A genuine cry enough, if from the wrong mouth.

The excuses of ignorance and necessity, however, as Father
Parsons well knew, would not avail with many Protestant readers,
even two years after the Commotion and the Powder Plot. There
was one other thing he could say.

'Some other false companion . . . is thought to have byn set a worke to induce them into that trap, as since hath byn understood'.[41]

No more. The *agent provocateur* defence indicated, and left. Parsons was probably concerned in 1606 to mention Allensmore only because Hamond had gone on record against it. The comfort of the faithful demanded refutation. In all other respects the Herefordshire commotion had been overshadowed by a later and greater disaster.

There is, however, one other document, dated March 1, 1607 and found amongst the Stonyhurst Collection,[42] which attempts to describe and explain the violent aftermath of the burial of Alice Wellington. Almost certainly later than the account of Father Parsons, it also alleges, a little more expansively, the presence of an *agent provocateur*. 'It was found on investigation', asserts the manuscript, 'that the disturbance had been raised and fomented by the treacherous designs of a certain Catholic, acting under the instigation of the heretics, who thus sought to render the Catholics more odious, and to furnish a pretext for persecuting them.' In pursuit of this aim the shadowy governmental villain next hurried on the printing of pamphlets, and lo! there was created immediately 'this great Herefordshire rebellion'.

This takes us very little farther. Indeed, of greater interest is a postscript, reputedly of fact, intended towards the greater exoneration of the Catholics of the March. After the rescue of Leonard Marsh, the document continues, so alarmed were the local inhabitants, 'although generally well inclined towards the Catholic religion', that 'they requested that the leading Catholics of London, such as the Archpriest with some of his reverend assessors, or the Jesuit Fathers and others, who possessed more authority over the Catholics, should immediately send some gentlemen into those parts with full authority to assist in allaying the excitement'. This, by the account, was done.

There are two points about this that deserve attention: first, the author's determination to underline the essentially correct behaviour and the sense of responsibility innate in the *Jesuited* party:

second, the clear implication that the Earl of Worcester arrived at the request of the Archpriest and the Jesuits and made the settlement he did with the full support of the responsible (i.e. Jesuited) Catholics of the district. It is not unreasonable to feel that the suspicions already entertained of him are confirmed.

The *agent provocateur* defence deserves little attention. There were only three persons at whom the allegation of treachery could with any show of reason be aimed: these were John Smith, Rice Griffiths and James Jones. The first, who admittedly had twice played his fellows false, appears to have been in prison for most of the vital period. James Jones, whatever his part may really have been, was, in view of his previous association with Fathers Jones and Powell, an unlikely mark for Jesuit arrows. There was also the awkward fact of his letter to Father Cresswell in Madrid, a document long since in Popham's hands. No, James Jones was not the man to whom a Jesuit apologist would feel it wise to draw attention. If, then, Rice Griffiths was intended, as seems probable, he is in no need of hasty defence.

Griffiths was commonly believed to have a special understanding with Archbishop Bancroft, and indeed boasted of it. Still under the guise of apostasy, he had in the twelve months previous to the commotion taken up again his priestly functions;[43] since King James came in he had used his access to the Bishop of Hereford to give warning of danger to his co-religionaries, and kept Roger Cadwallader supplied with books and other necessities. So much the confessions of deflated Catholics revealed at Griffiths's examination before Paul Delahay. No doubt he was one of the less reputable hangers-on of the anti-Spanish party, not fit to be named in the same breath as Roger Cadwallader or those who sought to strike an honest bargain with the Archbishop. No doubt he may never be mentioned with pride in Catholic annals. But on a graver charge there should be acquittal. That Griffiths was double-crossing Bancroft is likely. That he was treacherous to the Catholic cause in anything but outward show remains improbable and unproven.

Indeed, among the testimonies of so many little men clearing
themselves by setting a thicket or two more for the scapegoat,
there were very few which in any respect answered the real needs
of the Jesuit apologists. Griffiths was undoubtedly overimpressed
with his own cleverness, and there may have been others besides
John Smith who found his claim to have 'absolute intelligence in
State matters' intolerable.⁴⁴ Much was made of the publicity he had
given, both by letter and word of mouth, to hopes of toleration in
1603, and Smith alleged that he, Rice Griffiths, and not Cadwallader, was the author of the pre-Whitsun manifesto received by
the justices.⁴⁵ Harry Tailor, a minor participant in the Allensmore
burial, alleged that Griffiths either planned it or knew of it beforehand: Lewis Watkins of Kivernoll and William Caunt of Madley
swore that since the outbreak of violence he had sought to hearten
frightened Catholics by saying that the Archbishop of Canterbury
could be relied upon to minimize the affair. John Smith, however,
whose personal animosity was manifest, was the only one well
enough versed in political trickery either to make the kind of
charge which would seriously involve Rice Griffiths in responsibility for the riot or to seek, by fair means or foul, to undermine
his credit with the Archbishop.⁴⁶ His testimony, pointed as it was,
was probably much less impressive than he could have wished, if
only because Paul Delahay and any others his hearers well knew
that he had been absent from the county for much of the time
relevant. None of the simpler witnesses, in any case, was able to
allege that Griffiths misled his fellows by insisting that toleration
existed in 1605. Nor is an attempt to use his inside knowledge of
the Archbishop's likely attitude to put the best face on a dis-
couraging and frightening situation, disorder and riot having
already taken place, in any respect the same thing as an incitement
to violence. The charge of provocation goes wide of its mark.

William Morgan, be it noted, threw the blame on James Jones,
and appeared to mention Griffiths with reluctance. Apart from the
statement that the latter was to act as go-between to palliate the
affair in London, and that he was the *Magog* of the letters,

Morgan's confession avoided implicating him. But it is difficult to
attach any real weight to this. Morgan knew to whom he could
look for help, and to alienate the Archbishop by making Rice
Griffiths responsible for the outbreak would have been a poor way
to freedom.

Perhaps the strongest evidence in favour of the guilt of Rice
Griffiths is the total absence of his name from the pages of *The
Late Commotion*. A parallel of sorts may have existed between the
official tactics here and those discernible after the later and greater
plot of 1605, when the *King's Book* was brought out.[47] But this is a
very silent bough on which to hang an argument. Rice Griffiths is
in the wood at all only because he was a cause of contention between Dr. Bennett and the Archbishop. It is natural enough that
Catholic apologists, aware that the recusancy fines, though excuse
enough in August 1605, would not suffice for counter-attack on
the horrors of the Powder Plot, should have sought to make of his
double-dealing a further justification. Neither he nor John Smith
had any reputation among Catholics to lose.

Explanation, therefore, there is none from either side. What
spurred on William Morgan and his men to violence, whether it
was a judgment of assize, personal grievance, secret demagogy,
plain miscalculation of the times, or all of these together, may
never be known.

NOTES

[1] *History of England*, Vol. VII, pp. 540–1.
[2] E.g. *The Early Stuarts*, by Godfrey Davies, pp. 202–3: or S. R. Gardiner's
History of England, 1603–1642, Vol. I, pp. 97–100.
[3] *S.P.* 14, Vol. XIV, 40.
[4] *The Autobiography of an Elizabethan*. London, 1951.
[5] 'Welsh Catholics on the Continent', in Trans. Cymmrodorion 1901–2,
p. 79, note 2.
[6] *Historical Essays* (1957): 'Twice Martyred', pp. 113–18.

7 *Cal. of Salis. MSS.*, Pt. XII, pp. 631–2.

8 Letter signed by George Lambton, dated November 2, 1610. Printed in Foley, op. cit., Vol. IV, pp. 391–2.

9 Father Jones's account. Ibid., p. 391.

10 Sentence of death was relatively unusual: Cadwallader's demand for banishment, in the terms of the proclamation, was widely believed to have been refused because, using his well-known talent for controversy, he denied Bishop Bennett's episcopacy, disputed with him in Court, and 'put him to open shame'. *Vide* Father Jones, ibid., p. 389, and George Lambton, ibid., pp. 391–2.

11 *S.P.* 14, Vol. XIV, 40.

12 Bradney, *The Diary of Walter Powell*, p. 35, note 3, asserts that Edward Poyntz settled in Penrhos on his marriage to Florence, daughter of John Jones of Treowen. The date of this is not stated. But Poyntz was at Treget in 1603 (Duncumb, op. cit., *Hundred of Wormelow*, Lower Division, Pt. II, p. 30) and 1604 (*S.P.* 14, Vol. XIV, 53).

13 *S.P.* 14, Vol. XIV, 40.

14 *Cal. of Salis. MSS.*, Pt. XVII, p. 408. August 1605.

15 Besides one to John Smith, who may not yet have been clapped into the Gatehouse. *S.P.* 14, Vol. XIV, 45.

16 Ibid. The Earl of Worcester, on July 5, said that opinion locally was that he had in fact gone up to London. *Cal. of Salis. MSS.*, Vol. XVII, p. 305.

17 Third son of Richard Mynors of Treiago, St. Weonards, and married to Katherine, daughter of Thomas Gilbert of Dulas. *Llyfr Baglan*, p. 334. He had been indicted in Elizabeth's reign for harbouring seminary priests. Duncumb, op. cit., *Hundred of Wormelow*, Lower Division, Pt. I, p. 66.

18 Lingard, op. cit., Vol. VII, pp. 540–1, cited by Dodd, *Wales and the Scottish Succession*, p. 221.

19 The list of 'sojourners', like the other lists, presumably dated at least from Christmas 1604.

20 Gillow, *Biographical Dictionary of English Catholics*, Vol. II, pp. 324–5.

21 Report of a spy to Cecil in 1601. *Cal. of S.P. Dom. Eliz.*, xxxiv, Addenda.

22 There are grounds for believing that the Mrs. Elizabeth Morgan of Eaton Bishop, at whose house Rice Griffiths was alleged to have celebrated mass, was the widowed mother of Sir Charles Morgan, born Elizabeth Griffiths of Penmark. On the other hand, a deed of 1617 (*Mynde Collection*, No. 221) indicates that Elizabeth Morgan was then resident at Arkston.

23 William Morgan 'Being demaunded if Jones be come up to London he saith he thinketh he is, because he promised'. *S.P.* 14, Vol. XIV, 45.

24 Father John Gerard, in his narrative (op. cit. p. 45) described him as 'a very learned and remarkable man' and the co-worker of Father Oldcorne. Significantly, however, he gave him no further space, while of Oldcorne, the zealous preacher and ascetic, he had a great deal to say.

25 Gillow, op. cit., Vol. IV, p. 280. The correct title of this pamphlet of twelve pages, published in 1598, was *Adversus Factiosos in Ecclesia*. No separate printed copy is now known to exist, but there is a MS. copy among the Petyt MSS. in

the Inner Temple Library, and a printed copy incorporated in Dr. Christopher Bagshawe's *Relatio Compendiosa*.

²⁶ Ibid. In 1597 Garnet had written to the Father-General of Lister 'I am much annoyed and in a state of doubt and anxiety what to do with him'.

²⁷ Ibid. Watson's longest work, published in 1601, was entitled *A Decacordon of Ten Quodlibeticall Questions concerning Religion and State*.

²⁸ Ibid. Cresswell's complicity is quoted on the authority of Watson's *Quodlibets*. Jones's name appears to be added by Gillow.

²⁹ *Cal. of Salis. MSS.*, Pt. XVII, pp. 500–1. Thomas Wilson to E. of Salisbury, Nov. 20, 1605, but the notes are of Jesuit haunts 'a good while since'.

³⁰ In 1621 he was at last Superior of the Residence of St. Mary (the Oxford district) and died between 1625 and 1628. Foley, op. cit., Vol. VII, Pt. I, p. 462.

³¹ Salisbury's unwillingness to press the case against *messengers* was obviously based on Chief Justice Popham's earlier report.

³² *Cal. of Salis. MSS.*, Pt. XVIII, p. 36.

³³ Popham's information. *Cal. of Salis. MSS.*, Pt. XVII, pp. 395–6. Confirmed by William Morgan in his confession, *S.P.* 14, Vol. XIV, 45.

³⁴ If the pamphlet was officially sponsored, to be effective it had to appear before the news of the Gunpowder Plot became common knowledge. This again presupposes that the Council (or part of it) knew of the Powder Plot some time before its actual disclosure (*vide* Hugh Ross Williamson, op. cit., *passim*).

³⁵ *The Late Commotion*, p. B.3. This was Hamond's digest of the Lord Chancellor's version of the royal attitude.

³⁶ Thomas Hamond twice repeated the King's reported avowal that if any of his children, outliving him, changed or wished to change the Church as by law established, he would rather that they pre-deceased him.

³⁷ *A brief of the examinacons taken against Rice Griffiths als Williams a seminary priest*.

³⁸ Parsons, op. cit., p. 8.

³⁹ Ibid, p. 7.

⁴⁰ Ibid, p. 5.

⁴¹ Ibid, p. 6.

⁴² Father Grene's Collection C., printed in Foley, op. cit., Vol. IV, pp. 452–3.

⁴³ John Smith deposed that Griffiths 'hath lately contynued' the exercise of his priestly functions. He said mass about August 1604 and heard Smith's confession. Evan Price deposed that he had been saying mass at Mrs. Elizabeth Morgan's house at Eaton Bishop since Easter 1605. Nothing of this sort was alleged for any time earlier, save that at Michaelmas 1603 Griffiths married two recusants in the house of John Smith. *A brief of the examinacons taken against Rice Griffiths als Williams a seminary priest*. *Salisbury Papers*, available in MS. only. The heads of the examination are given in *Cal. of Salis. MSS.*, XVII, pp. 455–6.

⁴⁴ *A brief of the examinacons* . . . John Philipps's evidence.

⁴⁵ This may conceivably have referred to another letter: the actual entry reads: 'He confessed (in scorne) that he had cozened the Byshops by a letter from Cadwallader.' *A brief of the examinacons* . . .

46 *Vide* the allegation that Griffiths 'sayd he would preserve it for a tricke to stoppe the Byshop of Cant. mouthe if ever he came into any question'. Ibid.

47 The official title of this was *His Majesties Speach in this last Session of Parlia-ment ... together with a Discourse of the maner of the discovery of this late intended treason* (1605). *Vide* Hugh Ross Williamson, *The Gunpowder Plot*, p. 17.

CHAPTER IX

The Unquiet Hundreds

IF there is one task more than another which may yet illuminate a little the springs of action, it is to examine the peculiar and perhaps uniquely troublesome part played by the Hundreds of Webtree and Wormelow, together with the adjacent regions of south-west Herefordshire and the Monmouthshire border, between 1600 and 1606. There can be no pretending that this brings any nearer an immediate solution of the problems discussed in previous chapters, but it may perform some service in indicating what may be sought and argued in the future.

Bishop Mathew has written extensively[1] of 'the Essex country' – and in his sense of the words was not Archenfield the very home ground of the Devereux?[2] – pointing out that the protection afforded by the Earl in his lifetime against fines for recusancy was the invisible cord of allegiance binding Catholics to him. At least one of his generalizations, however, is wide of the mark. 'The Herefordshire squires', he wrote, 'lived in a world infinitely remote from affairs, since they were accustomed to stay on their lands, and the prosperity of their orchards and fields gave them employment, unlike that bare hill manor soil which drove the Welsh to the capital'.[3] After acknowledging the existence of obstinate Papists like Sir Roger Bodenham of Rotherwas and John Seabourne of Sutton St. Michael, he concluded, nevertheless, that 'there was no group among whom [Sir Gelly] Meyrick[4] laboured who would have proved less hopeful for his master's cause, for in Herefordshire they had prosperity and not even the Civil Wars disturbed their quiet acres'.[5] A shire in its entirety, however, is an ill subject upon which to generalize. What may conceivably have been true of eastern and central Herefordshire lingers oddly in the ear that has caught the frequency of the whisperings and scurryings in the Wye valley above Sugwas and Eaton Bishop or the mutterings from Hungerstone, Dore and Wormbridge, where the Golden Valley stands open to the east. Instead of 'the windless calm of apple-heavy orchards'[6] there was the more disturbing sight of '300 leazers or gleaners in one gentleman's cornfield at once'.[7] Rowland Vaughan's Golden Valley was 'the richest, yet from want of employment, plentifullest of poor in the kingdom'.[8] East of Kilpeck, and particularly on the far side of the Worm brook, there were fatter fields and yeomen with the girth of acres about them. But westward and northward were uncertainties, lands which, if potentially part of a richer economy, shared some of the chronic poverty of the slopes of the Black Mountains.

It may well be doubted, too, whether the squires who lived in these hundreds were really as remote from affairs as Bishop Mathew would suggest. The many relatives, mainly Parrys and Vaughans, who had looked Londonwards for favour while Blanche Parry of New Court, Queen Elizabeth's bedchamber-woman, was alive, had not looked in vain. James Parry of Poston had been at Court as Master of the Buckhounds[9] until misfortune overtook him.[10] Rowland Vaughan had been schooled by his great-aunt in London and thereafter maintained his metropolitan contacts,[11] probably to his cost. The potency of this interest had undoubtedly waned before King James ascended the throne, but only to be succeeded by that of other local families. In 1605 John Hoskyns, a yeoman's son from Monkton in the parish of Llanwarne (no more than a couple of miles south-east of Kilpeck), had been twelve months in Parliament as Member for the City of Hereford. Scholar as he was and double Wykehamist as he had been, he was already one of the most active lawyers in the Commons, and among the multifarious tasks of his first year at Westminster had been service on the committee for the bill for disabling recusants. All this might have been of small moment if Hoskyns, lost in self-admiration in the company of Richard Martin, Thomas Coryate, John Donne, Ben Jonson and other wits of whom the Middle Temple made him free, had abandoned interest in and connection with his native county. But his wife continued to live in Widemarsh Street in Hereford, and by 1611 he owned land at Didley, by Treville Park. His purchase of Arkston, and then in 1621 of Moorhampton in the Golden Valley, brought him at last a prime territorial interest in a district he deeply loved.[12]

Nor does this exhaust the outside contacts of families resident in the immediate area of disturbance. Henry Parry, a grandson of William Parry of Wormbridge, after a distinguished career at Corpus Christi, Oxford, and a Chaplaincy to Queen Elizabeth, became Dean of Chester in 1605 and Bishop of Worcester five years later.[13] It is difficult to believe that occasional intelligences did not reach the local Parrys from this relatively elevated ecclesiastical source. At The Mynde, a short distance east of Kilpeck in the parish of Much Dewchurch, lived the Pyes, a family whose apparent *quietism* seems to have been the cover for a deal of shrewd financial management. As the Morgans of Arkston and the Vaughans of New Court and Whitehouse were on the way down, the first through incapacity and litigation, the second because of their grandiose attempts at land reclamation, the Pyes of The Mynde were rising, engrossing tithes and manors, buying office, and playing ultimately a not inconsiderable part at the Court of both James I and Charles I.[14] Walter, the elder son of Roger Pye, had been educated at Oxford and had qualified as a barrister in 1597; in 1599, being then of the Middle Temple, he had leased The Mynde to his mother, Bridget Pye, for her lifetime, and it is not clear precisely when he returned to begin that mysterious process of land-purchase, the capital for which his account-books do not explain.[15]

In the close neighbourhood of his demesne, in the parish of Orcop, Anthony Pembridge of Wellington, John Hoskyns's fellow-Member for Hereford City, was a considerable landholder. Farther south, the house of Treiago was represented at Court in the person of Henry Mynors, Sergeant of the Carriages. John Scudamore of Kentchurch had a great-uncle, Philip Scudamore, who was a lawyer of Lincoln's Inn, and through his mother, a daughter of Sir John Pollard, was the possessor of lands in Oxfordshire at Charlton-on-Otmoor and Nuneham Courtenay, as well as relatives enough in that vicinity.[16] Resident at Staple Inn in London, too, was John Ballard, eldest son and heir to John Ballard of Llanwarne, and at the Middle Temple were others with local connections in John Cockes and John Powell. The south-westerly hundreds had, it seemed, been unusually prolific of lawyers and were not devoid of other metropolitan connections.

Records of land purchases and leases in the vicinity of Treville show a surprising traffic in and out in the period immediately preceding 1605. Charles Rogers of Monkhall by Kivernoll, younger son of an increasingly prosperous yeoman family, had twenty years earlier been able to describe himself first as 'gent' and then as 'citizen and grocer of London'.[17] He continued, like other relatives of his, to own considerable lands in the neighbourhood. In 1577 William Campe, 'stacioner', was a Kilpeck resident, and in 1589 Thomas Bearebrande, goldsmith, became a tenant of land and a house called 'Ten Acres' in the same parish. Throughout the same period Reginald Hyegate of Chappell in Essex and Sudborne in Suffolk, as the residuary legatee of much of the formerly considerable estate of Sir John Seyntleger and his widow, travelled between Kilpeck and his other houses. East and west were not so isolated from each other as might have been surmised. Had not the horde of Catholic 'incomers', in any case, already excited notice? It is difficult, if not impossible, to hold that in 1605 the main national issues, political and religious, were not understood in Webtree and Wormelow. The evidence is too much to the contrary. Indeed, one of the causes of Catholic confusion in 1605 was the availability even for the poorer Catholics of two rival intelligence-mongers in the persons of Rice Griffiths and John Smith.

It is not readily conceivable, in any case, that the valleys of Dore

and Monnow could have been indifferent to the not-very-distant
microcosm of the Devereux-Cecil struggle, the bitter and un-
ceasing feud between Paul Delahay of Allt-yr-ynys in Walterstone and John Arnold of Llanthony. That this was mainly a
personal struggle cannot be denied. But Delahay was the steward
of the Cecil lands in Monmouthshire, and Arnold a fervent sup-
porter of the Essex design. As early as 1598 Edward Kemish, Rice
Kemish (whose wife Wilgiford was a daughter of Dr. William
Aubrey, 'the great civilian'),[18] Henry Billingsley and William
Baker (father of the subsequently celebrated Benedictine David
Baker) were all suggested by Sir William Periam, Chief Baron of
the Exchequer, for the sheriffdom of the County of Monmouth as
'without exception, and not . . . of kin, or allied to Mr. Arnalt or
the other side'.[19] Sir William was either ill informed or deliberately
of intent to undermine the Cecil influence in the county: each of
the four men named was subsequently[20] objected against as either
a relative or a creditor of Arnold or his wife. But the local animus
was there: we need not doubt that Cecil not merely expected such
information but felt it his business to keep the Arnold group from
county office. The intervention of Delahay, then, in the outbreak
of 1605 made its point only in so far as he was taken locally for
Cecil's personal representative. To suppose that such an issue was
not broadly understood in south-west Herefordshire is unrealistic.

Nevertheless it was not in this struggle that the men east of the
Black Mountains chose to engage. According to John Bird, informer and notary-public, only a few of the Herefordshire squires
were implicated in the rebellion of the Earl of Essex, 'being
matched with Sir Gelly and most inward with his secrets'.[21] Those
whom he named were Roger Vaughan of Clyro, Lieutenant of
Radnorshire and Justice of the Peace, Sir Roger Bodenham of
Rotherwas, John Seabourne of Sutton St. Michael near Hungerstone and Owen Morgan of Marden.[22] There is no difficulty, however, in drawing a clear distinction between Roger Vaughan, who
was certainly implicated, and Bodenham and Seabourne, whom
even John Bird, general accusation apart, could only indict to the

extent that 'their houses were ever places of refuge of traitorous priests'. Rumour nudged Vaughan in much deeper: it was common talk among the servingmen about Sir Gelly, when they were free of the mews of London, that Essex 'hath enow (of friends) in Herefordshire, Radnorshire and other as far as great Roger Vaughan goeth'.[23] Only his absence from London at the time of the revolt itself cast any doubt upon Vaughan's full complicity. As for Owen James, alias Morgan, he was evidently an agent of secondary and occasional status. James Price, a servant of the Meyricks, was prepared to testify, said John Bird, that 'one Owen James in Wales . . . was used by Sir Gelly Meyrick and his brother Sir Francis for a bad instrument in sundry unsound actions'.

Two observations may therefore be made. The first is that the influence of Roger Vaughan, a Radnorshire grandee in any case, was overbearing only at a point much higher up Wye than Sugwas: like that of John Arnold, his writ did not run at any distance from the mountains. Owen Morgan was not a man of connections or influence in Herefordshire; as far as can be discovered, he was an incursor from Wales. If, then, the Essex connection was not solely a Welsh one in origin, Sir Gelly's personality and friendships appear to have made it so. When the clash came, the Herefordshire squires, even those west of Wye, were not amongst the followers of Essex in London and there were no guilty movements amongst them afterwards. But that this caution had much to do with economic satisfactions at home may be severely doubted.

The second observation bears closely on this. John Bird alleged that 'letters procured from the Earl stopped the course of law' against Roger Bodenham and his fellows. Such was Sir Gelly's power 'as no judges at the Assizes could bring them under the laws'.[24] But this indebtedness was repaid privately to the extent of £400 or £500 yearly. In other words, the recusancy of the gentlemen of Herefordshire was one of the secret financial props of the Essex connection. That it was not necessarily of political and military assistance may reasonably be deduced from the contrast between inactivity in the valleys of Dore and Monnow in 1601 and

I

their obvious implication in subsequent Catholic plots. There can
be no doubt that recusancy was the motive force in these western
hundreds, not, as in Roger Vaughan's case, political ambition. Is it
likely that if the Essex hold on Herefordshire had been anything
more than a matter of Sir Gelly's financial management Sir
Herbert Croft, an avowed opponent of the Catholic party among
the gentry, would have been found among the Earl's supporters?

Accusation against the inhabitants of the Golden Valley, and
regions south and east of it, of serious participation in the Essex
revolt can therefore be discharged. But after 1601 there *was* movement. At the death of Queen Elizabeth, as has already been noted,
William Morgan, John Smith and North the priest allegedly tried
to persuade Charles Morgan of Arkston to rise in arms. It was at
this time too that William Morgan of Llantarnam (whether he be
the same William Morgan or no) attempted to obtain custody of
the armour of the county.

The reward of lukewarmness at Arkston was a knighthood and
freedom to serve the cause of recusancy in south-west Herefordshire with less honesty and more countenance. Some time in 1604
or early 1605[25] a commission of inquiry was sent to Herefordshire
to make a survey of the lands of recusants, with a view to obtaining for the Council an assessment exact enough for real check on
subsequent fines and forfeitures. 'The commissioners', asserted the
Bishop of Hereford, 'were men of the most suspected note . . . and
they impanelled a jury like themselves, and the verdict yielded
2s. per annum to His Majesty more than was found before in the
days of Queen Elizabeth.' No doubt this complaint, reminiscent
of others about the subsidy,[26] was directed against substantially the
same group as had incurred the vociferous complaint of Herbert
Croft in respect of the Baskerville lands. John Baskerville of
Eardisley, son of Humphrey Baskerville, High Sheriff of the
County in 1578 and 1584, had died on January 8, 1589, less than
two years after his father, leaving for heir a boy only two years
old.[27] It is worth noting, however, that the infant had for grand-
mother Elizabeth Scudamore of Holme Lacy and for aunt the re-

doubtable Bridget Bodenham of Rotherwas. The history of the
suit for wardship is obscure, but before the old Queen died
Herbert Croft had, by his own account, spent a year and some
£500 in obtaining a lease of the lands from the Court of Wards at
a rental of £80 per annum. But the wardship had been blocked
'by a fraudulent office' since John Baskerville's death and the main
contest developed over the disposition of the fourteen years'
arrears.[28] It was the intention of Charles Morgan and John
Berington,[29] who had been nominated for the sheriffdom, to petition for the total remission of the arrears, and meanwhile to prevent any movement in Croft's favour by objecting to the
counter-nomination of John Blount, one of Croft's supporters,
and by putting off the hearing of Croft's case. Once installed in
office, they intended to impanel a jury certain to return a verdict
favourable to young Humphrey Baskerville and his relatives. This
emergence, upon the issues of recusancy and loss of revenue from
lands (whether from recusancy or wardship), of a recognizable
party of gentry of Catholic sympathies or connections makes in-
adequate Professor Neale's conclusion, based solely on a consideration of the contests for Membership of Parliament and the
Deputy-Lieutenancy of the Shire, that there was a lack of com-
petition in the county's social structure.[30] Even in the repetitive
Croft-Coningsby wrestling-match, there were aspects other than
these.[31] It would be interesting, again, to know at whose represen-
tations Charles Morgan had been dubbed Knight in 1603,[32] within
a few weeks of the according of the same honour to Herbert
Croft.[33]

Plainly the Essex connection, while not binding tightly together
the recusant and *independent* factions (if the Croft party may *so* be
called) had at least silenced their potential enmity. The breaking of
that connection released recusancy as a separate force of some
strength, and by 1603 it began to manifest itself in the Plot of
'Watson the traytor', maliciously and pictorially described by
Father Parsons as 'so wrong shapen and of so bad and blinking an
aspect as he looketh nine ways at once'. The Bishop of Hereford
I*

declared in 1605 that 'the late Watson's intended treason . . . was in part hammered' in Herefordshire.[34] That contention has never been seriously examined. Nor can it be here. But a few straws may point the wind.

What *were* the connections of William Watson with the county? Durham-born, he had no network of relationships there on which to rely. It may be that the presence at Wormesley of members of the Gage family[35] made a local connection for Anthony Copley,[36] one of Watson's chief associates. But this is a very thin thread with which to tag the Herefordshiremen. The real bond was probably with Roger Cadwallader, already known to have been close to Watson's opinion politically, and, less probably, with Rice Griffiths. In 1605 the Bishop of Hereford alleged that it was 'insinuated that Cadwallador . . . and William Morgan were actors, and had their finger in the late Watson's intended treason'.[37] In Whitsun week 1603, a month or so before the plot finally broke into the feeblest of action, there had been a considerable concourse of Catholics, it was remembered, at Seabourne's house at Sutton St. Michael, and the air of jollity among them had caused some remark. The south-western hundreds, it was to prove, did indeed provide, albeit tardily, a handful of rebels in arms who, after the débâcle, sought to ride home unnoticed.

But their company, 'well appointed with pistols', had drawn the attention at Tewkesbury of one of Chief Justice Popham's agents, who had quietly inquired of a servant among them where they were riding to. With the answer, 'London', came the *sotto voce* comment, 'I pray God we break not our sheenes before we come back again'.[38] This uncertain crew apparently arrived too late for such action as there was and might well have got safely home again and kept close but for the fact that Popham, having dinner on the evening of July 18 with Richard Bancroft, then Bishop of London, discovered from him that two Herefordshiremen named Parry and Vaughan were implicated in the plot but were not known to have made any move. He then called to mind the information he had received about the party of horsemen at Tewkesbury, whose names had not previously suggested that they were treasonably engaged, and full guilt was immediately established.

Chief among the plotters now actively implicated was John Parry of Poston near Peterchurch, a few miles north both of Blackmoor and New Court, the son and heir of that James Parry, Master of the Buckhounds to Queen Elizabeth,[39] who had recently died in the Fleet prison.[40] His cousins, Parrys, Vaughans and Milbornes, were scattered widely over the borders of Herefordshire and Breconshire, and his younger half-brother, the better-known Blanche Parry (so called as a tribute to the reputation of his aged relative, Mistress Blanche Parry), not only became sheriff of the latter county in 1618,[41] but remarried into the family of the Morgans of Arkston and Blackmoor.[42] John Parry's companions were Richard Croft of Michaelchurch-on-Arrow, and Eaton Bishop[43] (who, despite his close relationship to Sir Herbert Croft and William Rudhall, was by reputation 'a notable thief')[44] and Richard Davies, who lived no more than a mile or so from Poston. John Scudamore of Kentchurch, who, although twenty-six years of age, had not yet succeeded to the full acreage of his patrimony, was not seen at Tewkesbury with the others, but subsequent developments, as well as confessions in London, revealed that he was privy to the plot.[45] A Vaughan was also named, but which it is impossible to determine.[46]

William Watson, when in custody later, insisted that many of his supporters in Wales had not arrived in the London region because of the hostility of the Jesuits.[47] A gentleman named Meredith whose seat was west of Abergavenny, was 'at Lanternum or elsewhere ... incensed by Holland the jesuit[48] most sore' against him.[49] Nevertheless, Watson had earlier told Anthony Copley, his fellow-conspirator, that 'if the action might take place (in Wales) thousands would be up and in it, but to draw numbers up to London his advisers gave him little likelihood'.[50] And so it proved. From west of the border only John Harries of Haverfordwest and some thirty followers finally appeared, with a message for Watson indicating the success of Father Jones's dissuasions.[51] Chief Justice

Popham revealed to Sir Robert Cecil in July that he had had an 'advertisement out of west parts' of Watson's design and that a Jesuit priest there had named two seminaries, Walwood and Roe,[52] as being participants. He concluded that 'the Jesuit faction have their practice afoot as well as the others, though carried with more secrecy, and so the more dangerous'. The pattern of 1605 was uncovered, it would seem, fully two years earlier.

Once the conspirators from Herefordshire were identified the hunt was quickly up. Richard Hyett, Sheriff of the County, was able on July 25 to report that he had arrested John Scudamore at his house in Kentchurch, which he had searched from top to bottom for papers, but without success, and having sent the prisoner to the Privy Council in the custody of Henry Kyrle, his under-sheriff, was pressing after John Parry and Richard Davies, the former of whom was not at Poston and would have to be watched for by special 'spials'.[53]

Before long, moreover, south-west Herefordshire was even more heavily involved. John Scudamore admitted, under Sir William Waad's examination in London, that Watson himself was in the area and had been at Kentchurch perhaps as late as July 15.[54] He was reputedly seeking refuge in Ireland,[55] and seeking it by the route along which he knew he could count on support and comfort. Of many who would not go to London there were some, undoubtedly, who would see that he was led to safety, and it is not surprising to find Rice Griffiths accused in 1605 of having been one of those who conducted the fugitive from hiding-place to hiding-place[56] by crooked roads to the west. But with so many magistrates on the watch progress was slow. On July 29 Watson was still at liberty, but as yet hardly in Wales. A day or so later he was seized.

The place of his apprehension is in some doubt: according to Aubrey, who was probably free of a good deal of Herefordshire tradition, he was taken 'in a field by the Hay in Herefordshire (or Brecknockshire – *vide* the mapp) by Mr. Vaughan':[57] but an account of the life of the well-known Benedictine, Father

Augustine Baker, by his *socio*, Father Leander Prichard,[58] has it that Watson, guided by a recusant named David Williams, had a conversation with David Baker (as he then was) at an inn in Abergavenny, and that the fugitive and his guide 'were gone but a little way out of the town' afterwards when, Williams having again gone into an alehouse to drink, Mr. Vaughan, a justice of the peace, and his brother passed by and noticed the stranger lingering in the roadway. Subsequent questioning made suspicion certainty, and Watson was taken firmly into custody.

The captor was almost certainly Harry Vaughan of Moccas, appointed Lieutenant of Brecon and Steward of the Lordships of Brecon and Dinas in Elizabeth's day and probably still occupying those offices. If Father Prichard is to be believed, accompanying him in this martial exercise was his brother, none other than Rowland Vaughan of Whitehouse, a little fresher from the Irish wars than in 1610, when he publicized his waterworks. A Welsh doggerel song in the hand of Thomas Powell, prisoner in the county gaol at Brecon in 1680, commemorates the bravery of Harry Vaughan and, laughably, as many as six of his relations, 'when old Bess died'. 'In vile spelling and worse poetry', as Theophilus Jones has it,[59] it tells how the inhabitants of the high lands came down with their billhooks to attack an unnamed castle, which the arrival of Vaughan and his valorous relatives saved after a brisk fight. It would be ridiculous indeed if this should prove to be an account of Vaughan's capture of William Watson, who was all but unaccompanied and so short-sighted that he was compelled to hold a paper right up to his eyes to read.[60] And yet there is nothing else in 1603 or thereabouts to which it can refer. Probably popular memory was entirely capable of telescoping, even thus farcically, the whole story of Watson's Plot (in local terms) from the bravadoes of the Parry gang to the last wretched espial somewhere between Abergavenny and Hay, and crediting it all, with the familiar medieval ring, to Harry Vaughan. Aubrey gave him his valediction from a sourer tradition: 'T'was observed that Mr. Vaughan did never prosper afterwards'.[61]

There is only one other point of significance in this story. William Watson in prison wrote out an appeal and sent it, not, as might have been expected, to his fellow-Catholic the Earl of Worcester, but to the Protestant William Herbert, Earl of Pembroke.[62] In this respect the prisoner and Rowland Vaughan apparently had something in common. Worcester seems not to have enjoyed the confidence of the English party among the Catholics, which an accusation of venality might suggest he should. Here again the Earl's mask is in no danger of slipping.

The valleys of Dore and Monnow, as we have now seen, could hardly have been more actively involved than they were in Watson's design and the only matter for surprise is that William Morgan cannot be more positively identified as a participant. Two years later their inhabitants were again in arms at Treville and The Darren. Whether the powerhouse of this continued militancy will ever be more than guessed at it is difficult to know. Certainly the search is worth a little persistence yet.

If these hundreds maintained their attachment to trouble into the later months of 1605, it was more fortuitously and as a result of the machinations of the *other* party. During the flight of the conspirators westward after the failure of the Gunpowder Plot, Father Hall the Jesuit allegedly approached Father Robert Jones to make arrangements to hide Robert Winter and Stephen Lyttleton at The Cwm, Llanrothal. George Charnock, a member of Humphrey Lyttleton's household at Hagley, Worcestershire, not far from which Winter and Stephen Lyttleton were seized, had been briefed to guide them to The Cwm.[63] On the miscarriage of the plan and the apprehension of the conspirators Humphrey Lyttleton and Charnock rode off at speed but did not get far before they were captured.[64] Subsequently a prisoner in Worcester Gaol, Charnock confessed 'with much ado' both to the plan and to the token by which he was to bring the fugitives to Father Jones, on whose head a price was then laid.

Whether the Jesuits Hall and Garnet were fully apprised beforehand of the design of the Gunpowder Plotters is a question sufficiently difficult. But evidence of Father Jones's foreknowledge is even harder to come by. It is perhaps significant that Humphrey Lyttleton should allege that the Welsh Jesuit was at the house of Robert Winter in Worcestershire when he was asked by his colleague Hall to shelter the conspirators.[65] Two sentences in Robert Abbot's *Antilogia*, published in 1613, appear to suggest that one of the Winters was active in support of the disturbances at The Darren, and was roundly cursed for showing his hand in a manner likely to jeopardize the Powder Plot.[66] No support for this allegation can be found in the State Papers or the Salisbury Papers as they relate to the commotion in Herefordshire and Monmouthshire, but Abbot, in 1613 both Master of Balliol and Regius Professor of Divinity at Oxford, was the official protagonist of the Protestant interest and because of the Council's determination that Eudaemon Joannes (the Jesuit L'Heureux) and his vindication of Garnet should be effectively answered, was, in Jardine's opinion,[67] given free access to all the documentary evidence in the government's possession.

Of such generalities, however, no argued connection between the Powder Plot and the Herefordshire outbreak can readily be made. Sir Edward Coke at Garnet's trial asserted that the prisoner, who had known of the Powder Plot since the midsummer of 1604, on hearing of 'certain broils in Wales' wrote immediately to the Pope requesting that either he or Aquaviva, the General of the Jesuits, should command the staying and silencing of all Catholic commotions, so that 'less impediment might be offered to this main plot by reason of any suspicion of the stirring of Papists, or of inquiry after them upon occasion of any petty commotions or broils'.[68] Later, when Garnet had admitted that he had been told at Whitsuntide 1605 by the Jesuit Greenwell[69] the full details of the Powder Plot, the Earl of Salisbury asked him why he could not as well have written to the Pope and Aquaviva to procure a prohibition of this as 'for other smaller matters'.[70] 'Garnet faintly answered, he might not disclose it to any, because it was matter of secret confession,[71] and would endanger the lives of divers men.'

Nothing much more to any purpose emerges, though there is in Popham's hand a breviat,[72] two of whose articles run as follows:

'Garnet knew of the Gunpowder Treason as himself saith about Whitsuntide 1605, and yet never acquainted the State with it whereby it might be prevented.

Though he saith he then dissuaded it, yet confesseth he was then inquisitive to know if the Catholics were then of force sufficient to oppose against the King, whereby he might advertise the Pope of it: *ergo*, he did not dissuade them in the other plot.

The prosecution were proposing to suggest, it would appear, that Father Garnet for a time considered the possibility of encouraging and maintaining both the Powder Plot and the Herefordshire Commotion, until such time at least as the general strength of Catholicism could be judged. If that should prove insufficient, it would then be the moment to stop 'by censures' the more open of the two, so that Catholics *en masse* should not suffer unnecessarily. Whatever the degree of truth behind this insinuation, it does not assist in deciding whether when censures were finally imposed on William Morgan and his friends, this was done because the Herefordshire outbreak was in genesis and personnel politically less welcome to the Jesuit hierarchy or merely because it was much less likely to succeed. By the same limits, it is not possible to estimate the validity of the more recent charge[73] that what happened at Allensmore and Treville and The Darren was played down by the Council, some of whom were well aware of Catesby's plans, in order not to spoil with preliminary cracklings the presentation to the public of the heinous and treasonable explosion which they intended presently to discover.

And so inquiry, having encountered a number of blank walls and dim, unlit corners, must come to a stop. It is always possible that there are more doors than the present light allows. If so, there will, sooner or later, be someone to go through them. Meanwhile it must be enough to have brushed up against a number of figures, some already well enough known to recognize, some new and only momentarily seen, and to have kept them awhile from a greater dark.

NOTES

[1] Chiefly in *The Celtic Peoples and Renaissance Europe*, 1933.

[2] Archenfield, traditionally the area around Ewyas Harold, was the district of origin of the Devereux family, to which the Earl of Essex belonged. Bishop Mathew, op. cit., p. 339, describes them as 'a family of Herefordshire squires, who had hoisted themselves by two strategical marriages'.

[3] Op. cit., p. 348.

[4] Steward to the Earl of Essex: a man with extensive lands in Radnorshire and on the March.

[5] David Mathew, op. cit., p. 349.

[6] Ibid.

[7] Rowland Vaughan, (ed. E. B. Wood) pp. 31–32.

[8] Ibid, p. 30.

[9] Theophilus Jones, op. cit., Vol. IV, pp. 1–3.

[10] He was a prisoner in the Fleet in 1593. *A Catalogue of Star Chamber Proceedings*, p. 25.

[11] C. A. Bradford, op. cit., p. 7.

[12] *The Life, Letters and Writings of John Hoskyns*, by L. B. Osborn. New Haven, N.Y., 1937, *passim*.

[13] *Athenae Oxonienses, I*, p. 415.

[14] Walter, the elder brother, was a barrister of the Middle Temple: by Buckingham's favour he was in 1617 made a justice for Glamorgan, Breconshire and Radnorshire, and in 1621 Attorney of the Court of Wards and Liveries. He was knighted in 1630. Robert, by similar favour, became Remembrancer of the Exchequer in 1618, was knighted in 1621, and ultimately represented Woodstock in the Long Parliament. *D.N.B. Vide* also *The King's Servants*, by G. E. Aylmer, pp. 308–10 for Walter Pye, pp. 311–13 *et passim* for Robert.

[15] Aylmer, op. cit., pp. 308–9.

[16] *Schedule of the Kentchurch Court Papers*.

[17] *Schedule of Mynde Park Documents*.

[18] *John Aubrey and his Friends*, Anthony Powell, table opp. p. 294.

[19] *Cal. of Salisbury MSS.*, XIV, p. 81.

[20] The Calendar is undoubtedly out of order here: the document on p.45 tentatively assigned to 1597 is plainly *post* November 1598.

[21] *Cal. of Salis. MSS.*, XI, p. 107.

[22] *S.P.* 14, Vol. XIV, 53. Owen Morgan and his wife were named in the Sheriff's List of 1604.

23 *Cal. of Salis. MSS.*, XI, p. 134.

24 *Cal. of Salis. MSS.*, XI, p. 107.

25 *Cal. of Salis. MSS.*, XVII, p. 235. Bishop of Hereford to Earl of Salisbury, June 1, 1605. He described the commission as arriving 'lately'.

26 *Vide*, for example, Sir Walter Raleigh's statement in the Parliament of 1593: 'Our Estates that be £30 or £40 in the queenes Books are not the hundredth part of our wealth.'

27 Robinson, op. cit., p. 106.

28 *Cal. of Salis. MSS.*, XV, p. 369.

29 *Cal. of Salis. MSS.*, XII, p. 499.

30 *The Elizabethan House of Commons*, pp. 34–5.

31 *Vide*, for instance, the immediate contest, on the demise of the Earl of Essex in 1601, for the vacant Stewardship of Leominster. Sir Robert Cecil recommended Herbert Croft, whose grandfather was Steward in his time, but this was immediately resisted by the Bailiff and Deputy-Recorder of the Borough, who had forwarded the election of Sir Thomas Coningsby, his inveterate opponent, who also had a hereditary claim to the office. *Cal. of Salis. MSS.*, XI, p. 114.

32 Bradney, op. cit., Vol. I, p. 278.

33 Dubbed at Theobalds, May 7, 1603. *A Book of Knights, 1426–1660*, by Walter C. Metcalfe (1885), p. 141.

34 *S.P.* 14, Vol. XIV, 52. Printed in Tierney's Dodd, Vol. IV, Appendix p. C.

35 Francis Gage and his wife, the former indicted for his presence at mass in John Ireland's house in Hereford February 2, 1604, and the latter included in the list of the 'principall and most dangerous Recusants' at Christmas 1604. *S.P.* 14, Vol. XIV, 53.

36 *Cal. of Salis. MSS.*, XV, p. 221. From this it appears that Copley's sister was the wife of John Gage, the Archpriest Blackwell's messenger. Copley was to be interrogated (July 1603?) as to 'what speeches he had with his sister Gadge'. There were, however, other Gages than John to whom this relationship could point. After the Babington Plot of 1589 both an Edward and a John Gage were held in custody, together with Katherine Copley, widow, and her daughter Margett. Pubs. Catholic Record Society, Miscellanea, II, pp. 257–69. The juxtaposition of 'Mr. Gaige' and Thomas Abington in the Tower suggests a Herefordshire connection. *Ibid.* pp. 257–8.

37 *S.P.* 14, Vol. XIV, 52.

38 *Cal. of Salis. MSS.*, XV, p. 201.

39 John was his father's eldest son by his unnamed first wife, and himself had married Mary Leighton of Shropshire. Theophilus Jones, op. cit., Vol. IV, p. 3. It is not clear why Prof. Dodd should refer to an 'unidentified Mr. Parry'. *Wales and the Scottish Succession*, p. 215. James Parry, the father, had been a somewhat distant cousin to Blanche Parry, who for so long ruled Queen Elizabeth's bedchamber. Despite the separation of blood, however, he became in 1582 a beneficiary under her will.

40 *Cal. of Salis. MSS.*, XV, p. 393. In 1593 he brought an action from the Fleet

against Roger Bodenham of Rotherwas, Roger Vaughan and others, over the marriage portion of his second wife, the daughter of John Morgan of Brecon. *Catalogue of Star Chamber Proceedings*, p. 25.

⁴¹ Bradney, op. cit., Vol. I, p. 278.

⁴² Blanche Parry married Anne, the daughter of Thomas Morgan of Black-moor. Ibid. Also Theophilus Jones, op. cit., p. 3. Clark, however, in his *Limbus Patrum*, insisted that this Thomas Morgan was Sir Charles Morgan of Arkston's younger brother, and that Anne was therefore his niece. Blanche can be said to have *remarried* into the Morgans because his mother, Joan Morgan (or Games) was descended both from the Gam family of Newton, Brecon, and from the Morgans of Arkston. If Clark is to be depended upon (op. cit., p. 258) she was first cousin to James Morgan, Sir Charles's grandfather.

⁴³ He had married, some ten years before, the widow of Hakluyt of Eaton Bishop. *Cal. of Salis. MSS.*, XV, pp. 201 and 393.

⁴⁴ Ibid. Richard Croft was the plaintiff in an action of 1606, in which he protested, amongst other things, that he had been wrongfully indicted of rape. *Catalogue of Star Chamber Proceedings*, p. 213.

⁴⁵ *Cal. of Salis. MSS.*, XV, p. 210.

⁴⁶ Prof. Dodd refers (*Wales and the Scottish Succession*, p. 215) to Captain Vaughan, a brother of Sir John Vaughan of Golden Grove, but the authority for this does not appear.

⁴⁷ Copley's declaration, Lingard, op. cit., Vol. VII, p. 539.

⁴⁸ Father Robert Jones.

⁴⁹ Tierney's Dodd, Vol. IV, Appendix No. 1, p. xxxv.

⁵⁰ Ibid. p. v.

⁵¹ Ibid. p. xxxv.

⁵² 'a Devonshire man'. *Cal. of Salis. MSS.*, XV, p. 202.

⁵³ Ibid. p. 210.

⁵⁴ On July 29 it was 'within these three weeks' and (Sir William Waad thought) 'within lesser time'. Ibid., pp. 213–14.

⁵⁵ Cath. Record Society Publications, Vol. XXXII, p. 81.

⁵⁶ *A brief of the examinacons . . . Cal. of Salis. MSS.*, XVII, pp. 455–6.

⁵⁷ *Brief Lives*, p. 161.

⁵⁸ Cath. Record Society Publications, Vol. XXXII. 'The Second Treatise,' p. 81.

⁵⁹ Op. cit., Vol. I, p. 119.

⁶⁰ D.N.B.

⁶¹ Op. cit., p. 161.

⁶² D.N.B.

⁶³ *Cal. of Salis. MSS.*, XVIII, pp. 35–36.

⁶⁴ Ibid. p. 17.

⁶⁵ Ibid. p. 35.

⁶⁶ P. 131. 'Sed erat inde alter adhuc motus periculosior ad vicum Darren in eodem Herefordiensi comitatu, quo instigantibus Sacerdotibus quibusdam vestris turba vestrorum magis numerosa confluxit; quo armati concurrere

coeperant & apertam minitari perduellionem graveque aliquod malum parturire visi sunt, altero tum e Winteris *deuouente diris mancipia, quibus tam praeceps furor ut animi sui ante tempus indicia darent* . . . Quorum furoribus compescendis missae quoque tum, opinor, Archipresbyteri literae, sed tantum eo fine ut postea patebit, quod & Winteri execratio manifestum facit, ne intempestiva seditio pulvereo negotio impedimento esset.'

[67] *A Narrative of the Gunpowder Plot.* (London, 1857) p. 278. George Abbot, Archbishop of Canterbury, was the pamphleteer's brother, and there is extant among the State Papers a memorandum stating that many of the documents relating to the plot were in the Archbishop's possession between October 9, 1612 and July 1, 1614 (when they were returned), a period which covers the composition of the *Antilogia*.

[68] *State Trials*, Howells, p. 230.

[69] Father Oswald Tesmond, alias Greenway.

[70] Howells, op. cit., p. 240.

[71] Sir Edward Coke's reply to this was (i) that it was not a sacramental confession and the teller was not penitent; (ii) that it was a thing in the future, not the past; (iii) that Greenwell told it not of himself but of others, and that therefore he could have revealed the mischief but concealed the persons; (iv) that Catesby had told him earlier *extra confessionem.* Howells, op. cit., p. 245.

[72] *Cal. of Salis. MSS.*, XVIII, p. 76.

[73] Hugh Ross Williamson, op. cit., *passim.*

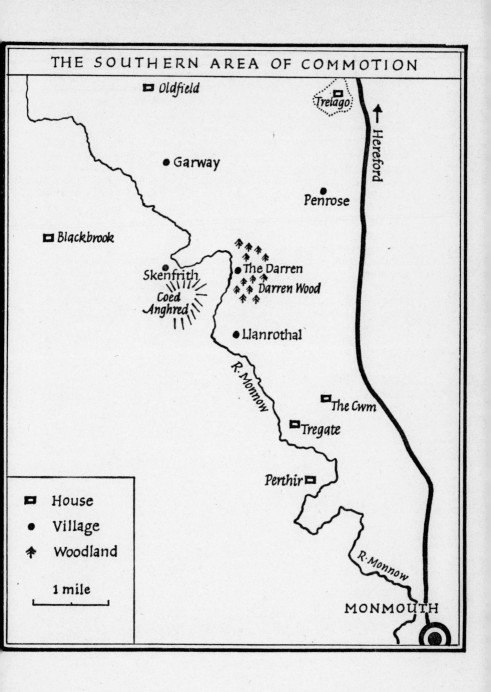

THE SOUTHERN AREA OF COMMOTION

Oldfield

Treiago

Hereford

Garway

Penrose

Blackbrook

Skenfrith

The Darren

Darren Wood

Coed
Anghred

Llanrothal

R. Monnow

The Cwm

Tregate

Perthir

R. Monnow

MONMOUTH

House

Village

Woodland

1 mile

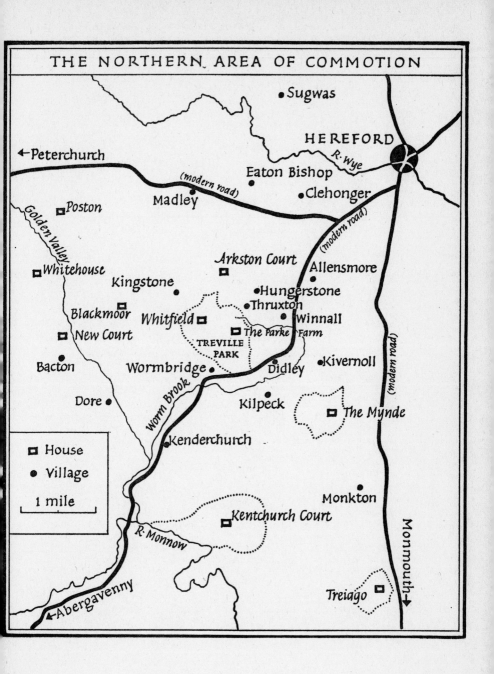

THE NORTHERN AREA OF COMMOTION

Sugwas

HEREFORD

R. Wye

← Peterchurch

Eaton Bishop

(modern road)

Madley

Clehonger

Poston

Golden Valley

Whitehouse

Arkston Court

Allensmore

(modern road)

Kingstone

Hungerstone

Thruxton

Blackmoor

Whitfield

Winnall

New Court

The Parke

Farm

TREVILLE PARK

Bacton

Wormbridge

Didley

Kivernoll

Worm Brook

Dore

Kilpeck

The Mynde

☐ House

● Village

1 mile

Kenderchurch

Monkton

Kentchurch Court

R. Monnow

Treiago

← Abergavenny

Monmouth →

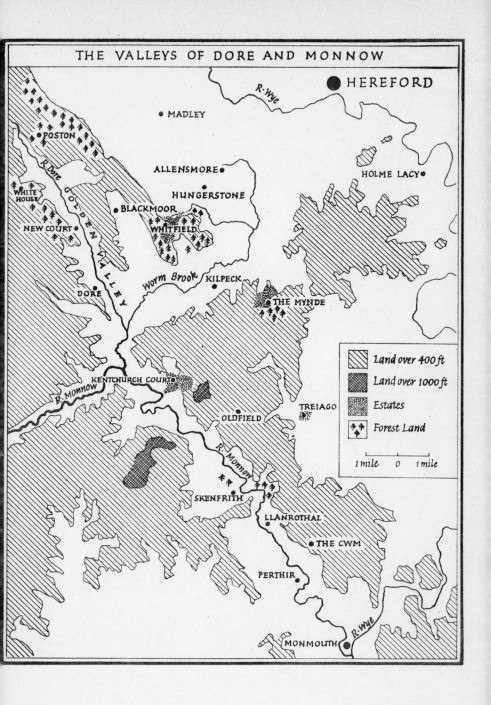

THE VALLEYS OF DORE AND MONNOW

HEREFORD

R. Wye

MADLEY

POSTON

R. Dore

WHITE
HOUSE

NEW COURT

ALLENSMORE

HOLME LACY

HUNGERSTONE

GOLDEN VALLEY

BLACKMOOR

WHITFIELD

DORE

Worm Brook

KILPECK

THE MYNDE

KENTCHURCH COURT

R. Monnow

OLDFIELD

TREIAGO

R. Monnow

SKENFRITH

LLANROTHAL

THE CWM

PERTHIR

R. Wye

MONMOUTH

Land over 400 ft

Land over 1000 ft

Estates

Forest Land

1 mile   0   1 mile

Bibliography

A list of the authorities used:

1. Manuscript Sources:

Abergavenny MSS., No. 1. [Rental of Manors in Wales 15 Jan. 28 Eliz.], National Library of Wales.

Arnott MSS., No. 15. [Boundary of the Manor of Monmouth, 1610], National Library of Wales.

Detecta in Vis, Book 82, Episcopal Archives, Hereford, (for 1605).

Garway, MS. No. 2464, Hereford City Library. [The Darrein, &c., 1698].

Inquisitiones Post Mortem, Vol. III, James I. Public Record Office.

Local Collection, MS. No. 3408, Hereford City Library.

Pilley Collection, Drawer 2, No. 8, Hereford City Library.

Star Chamber Proceedings, James I. Bundles I–X. Public Record Office.

State Papers Domestic of the Reign of James I. Vols. XIV, XXXII and XLIX.

2. Printed Sources:

(a) CALENDARS AND SCHEDULES

The Calendar of the Manuscripts of The Marquis of Salisbury, preserved at Hatfield House. Parts IX, X (1904), XI (1906), XII (1910), XIV (1923), XV (1930), XVI (1933), XVII (1938), XVIII (1940). (Some of the documents calendared were consulted in manuscript.)

The Calendar of State Papers, Domestic, James I, Vols. XII–XV. London, 1857.

The Calendar of State Papers, Venetian, Vol. X, 1603–7. London, 1900.

A Catalogue of Star Chamber Proceedings relating to Wales. Compiled by Ifan ab Owen Edwards. Cardiff, 1929.

A Catalogue of MSS. relating to Wales in the British Museum (Cymmrodorion Record Series, No. 4).

Crosby Records: A Chapter of Lancashire Recusancy, ed. Rev. T. E. Gibson. Chetham Society, 1887. (In particular the *Introduction* by Rev. Alexander Goss.)

Exchequer Proceedings Concerning Wales in tempore James I, compiled by T. G. Jeffreys Jones. Cardiff, 1955.

The Manuscripts of Hereford Corporation, Historical Manuscripts Commission, Thirteenth Report, Appendix, Part IV. London, 1892.

A Schedule of the Kentchurch Court Papers and Documents, compiled by B. G. Owens, Vol. I [Typescript], National Library of Wales, 1957.

A Schedule of the Mynde Park Deeds and Documents, compiled by B. G. Charles. Vol. I [Typescript], National Library of Wales, 1960.

(*b*) OTHER CONTEMPORARY DOCUMENTS, NOW PRINTED

The Diary of Walter Powell 1603–1654, ed. J. A. Bradney. Bristol, 1907.

Extracts from Blount [of Orleton]'s MSS. Collections for A History of Herefordshire, made by Rev. John Webb of Tretire. Hereford City Library.

John Gerard, *The Autobiography of an Elizabethan*, translated and edited by Philip Caraman. London, 1951.

Illustrations of British History, Biography and Manners in the reigns of Henry VIII, Mary, Elizabeth and James I [Howard, Talbot and Cecil MSS.], by Edmund Lodge. London, 1791.

Llyfr Baglan, 1600–1607 [by John Williams], transcribed from the original MS. and edited by J. A. Bradney. London, 1910.

Memoirs of Affairs of State in the Reigns of Queen Elizabeth and King James I, collected from the original papers of Sir Ralph Winwood. Vol. II., 1725.

Memorials of Father Augustine Baker and other documents relating to the English Benedictines, edited by Dom Justin McCann and Dom Hugh Connolly O.S.B. Publications of the Catholic Record Society, Vol. XXXIII.

State Trials, Vol. II, edited by T. B. Howell. London, 1816.

William Weston, The Autobiography of an Elizabethan, translated from the Latin by Philip Caraman. London, 1955.

(*c*) CONTEMPORARY PRINTED BOOKS

Robert Abbot, *Antilogia Adversus Apologiam Andreae Eudaemon-Joannis Iesuitae pro Henrico Garneto*. London, 1613.

John Gwillim, *A Display of Heraldrie*. London. Printed by William Hall for Raphe Mab, 1611.

[Thomas Hamond], *The Late Commotion of certaine Papists in Herefordshire*, Imprinted at London by S. Stafford for I. Chorlton and F. Burton, 1605.

P. R. [Robert Parsons], *A Treatise tending to Mitigation towardes Catholicke Subiectes in England*. 1607.

Rowland Vaughan, *Most Approved and Long Experienced Waterworkes, Containing the Manure of Winter and Summer Draining of Meadow and Pasture*. Imprinted at London by George Eld, 1610.

(d) Printed Sources of More Recent Date

Anon, *A Short Narrative of the Discovery of a College of Jesuits at . . . The Come.* London, 1679.

John Aubrey, *Brief Lives and Other Selected Writings*, edited by Anthony Powell. London, 1949.

G. E. Aylmer, *The King's Servants.* London, 1961.

C. A. Bradford, *Blanche Parry, Queen Elizabeth's Gentlewoman.* London, 1935.

C. A. Bradford, *Rowland Vaughan: An Unknown Elizabethan.* London, 1937.

J. A. Bradney, *A History of Monmouthshire.* Vols. I–III. London, 1904–23.

John Britton, *The History and Antiquities of the Cathedral Church of Hereford.* London, 1831.

J. H. Canning, *Bl. John Kemble.* Catholic Truth Society publication (date unnoted).

Bishop Challoner, *Memoirs of Missionary Priests, &c. (1577–1784).* Manchester, 1803.

G. T. Clark, *Limbus Patrum Morganiae et Glamorganiae.* London, 1886.

O. G. S. Croft, *The House of Croft of Croft Castle.* Hereford, 1949.

Godfrey Davies, *The Early Stuarts, 1603–1660.* Oxford, 1937.

The Dictionary of National Biography.

The Dictionary of Welsh Biography. London, 1959.

Dodd's *Church History of England*, edited and continued by the Rev. M. A. Tierney, Vol. IV. London, 1841.

M. B. Donald, *Elizabethan Monopolies: The History of the Company of Mineral and Battery Works from 1565 to 1604.* Edinburgh, 1961.

John Duncumb, *Collections towards the History and Antiquities of the County of Hereford* (Hereford, 1804), in particular the continuation by John Hobson Matthews, *Hundred of Wormelow* (1913).

A. Hugh Fisher, *The Cathedral Church of Hereford.* London, 1898.

Henry Foley, *Records of the English Province of the Society of Jesus*, Vols. IV and VII (Pts. I and II). London, 1878–82.

S. R. Gardiner, *History of England 1603–1642*, Vol. I. London, 1900.

John Gerard, *The Gunpowder Plot and the Gunpowder Plotters.* London, 1897.

Joseph Gillow, *Biographical Dictionary of the English Catholics*, Vol. II. London, 1880.

G. C. Harrison, *A Last Elizabethan Journal, 1599–1603.* London, 1933.

Christopher Hill, *The Century of Revolution, 1603–1714.* London, 1961.

M. Newton Jackson, *Bygone Days in the March Wall of Wales.* London, 1926.

David Jardine, *A Narrative of the Gunpowder Plot.* London, 1857.

Theophilus Jones, *A History of Brecknockshire.* Vols. I–IV. 3rd ed., revised. Brecon, 1909–11.

Ella M. Leather, *The Folk-lore of Herefordshire*. Hereford, 1912.

John Lingard, *The History of England from the first invasion by the Romans to the Accession of William and Mary*. 5th ed., Vol. VII. London, 1849.

J. P. Malcolm, *First Impressions*. London, 1807.

David Mathew, *The Celtic Peoples and Renaissance Europe*. London, 1933.

David Mathew, *Sir Tobie Mathew*. London, 1950.

Walter C. Metcalfe, *A Book of Knights, 1426–1660*. London, 1885.

J. E. Neale, *The Elizabethan House of Commons*. London, 1949.

Louise B. Osborn, *The Life, Letters and Writings of John Hoskyns, 1566–1638*. New Haven, 1937.

Edwin Poole, *The Illustrated History and Biography of Brecknockshire*. Brecknock, 1886.

Anthony Powell, *John Aubrey and His Friends*. London, 1948.

Rev. Charles J. Robinson, *A History of the Mansions and Manors of Herefordshire*. London, 1873.

Hugh Trevor-Roper, *Archbishop Laud, 1573–1645*. London, 1940.

Hugh-Trevor-Roper, *Historical Essays* (especially No. XVII: 'Twice Martyred'). London, 1957.

Penry Williams, *The Council in the Marches of Wales under Elizabeth I*. Cardiff, 1958.

Hugh Ross Williamson, *The Gunpowder Plot*. London, 1951.

Anthony à Wood, *Athenae Oxonienses*, together with *The Fasti* or Annals of the University of Oxford. Vol. I. London, 1721.

Ellen B. Wood, (ed.), *Rowland Vaughan his Booke*. London, 1897.

(*e*) ARTICLES IN PERIODICALS

Thomas Blashill, *Abbeydore*, in Transactions of the Woolhope Club, 1883–5.

J. M. Cronin, *The Legend of the Darren Brook*, St. Peter's Magazine, Cardiff, Vol. IV, No. 10, 1924.

A. H. Dodd, *Wales and the Scottish Succession*, Transactions of the Cymmrodorion Society, 1937.

A. H. Dodd, *Two Welsh Emigrés discuss the Accession of James I*, Bulletin of the Board of Celtic Studies, Vol. VIII, Part IV.

Rev. E. R. Firmstone, *The Origin of Kilpeck*, in Transactions of the Woolhope Club, 1912–13.

Iltyd Gardner, *The Church of Kilpeck, Herefordshire*, in Archaeologia Cambrensis, Vol. LXXXII, 1927.

George H. Marshall, *Some Account of Vowchurch*, in Transactions of the Woolhope Club, 1914–17.

John Hobson Matthews, *Records Relating to Catholicism in the South Wales Marches*. Publications of the Catholic Record Society, Vol. II, 1906.

John Hobson Matthews, *Tower Bills 1595–1681*, Publications cit. Vol. IV.

Rev. G. M. Metcalfe, *Peterchurch and its History*, in Transactions of the Woolhope Club, 1881–2.

Walter Pilley, *Notes on the Suppressed College of Jesuits at Combe*, in Transactions of the Woolhope Club, 1900.

Rev. J. H. Pollen, S.J. (ed.), *Official Lists of Catholic Prisoners during the Reign of Queen Elizabeth: Part II (1581–1602)*. Publications of the Catholic Record Society, Vol. II. 1906.

Rev. H. E. G. Rope, *John Davies of Hereford*, The Anglo-Welsh Review, Vol. 11 No. 28, 1961.

Penry Williams, *The Welsh Borderland under Queen Elizabeth*, The Welsh History Review, Vol. I No. I, 1960.

W. Llywelyn Williams, *Welsh Catholics on the Continent*, Transactions of the Cymmrodorion Society, 1901–02.

Index

145

Demco 38-297